FROM DARKNESS INTO LIGHT

Anthony Condon and John Broom

FROM DARKNESS INTO LIGHT

The War Heroes Who Helped Save Cricket from Oblivion

pitch

First published by Pitch Publishing, 2023

Pitch Publishing
9 Donnington Park,
85 Birdham Road,
Chichester,
West Sussex,
PO20 7AJ
www.pitchpublishing.co.uk
info@pitchpublishing.co.uk

A CIP catalogue record is available for this book from the British Library.

ISBN 978 1 80150 442 3

Typesetting and origination by Pitch Publishing

Printed and bound in Great Britain by TJ Books, Padstow

Contents

DEDICATIONS

From John

To Dawn, Rosa, Sophia and David. May your sporting values endure.

From Anthony

To the librarians and archivists around the world that made the research of this book possible, and to my family for their continued support.

Foreword

THE SHADOWS of the Great War hang over us to this day. In 2014, to commemorate the 100th anniversary of the outbreak of war, I produced a painting, *Seconds from Hell*, to honour the sacrifice of my great-great-uncle, Private Edward Hogg 7323, aged 28, who was serving with the 1st Battalion Gloucestershire Regiment.

He was killed on 7 November 1914, leaving a grieving wife in Stroud. Edward's permanent whereabouts remain unknown, and he is one of 55,000 missing men commemorated on the Menin Gate in Ypres.

I made a pilgrimage to the very field where he died. Edward, along with 300 of his Gloucestershire comrades, left the Belgian village of Zwartelen and never returned.

As a youngster I used to play by the war memorial which bears his name. In 2009 I found a photograph of

Edward which prompted me to consult the regimental war diaries.

I sat in a car by the field where he died at 9am, the precise time at which the battalion was ordered to advance to the woods. I then walked down the road to the spot where Edward Hogg and his comrades last breathed Earth's air.

It was hard to know what happened in that field but it was horrific. They lay out there all day, suffering. Some of them made it back under the cover of darkness. The accounts of that time are very moving. Of the 500 that went out that morning, only 200 came back.

It was strange to feel so emotional, even though I'd never met the guy. He was my family. I felt like I knew him and this was the closest I could get to him. It was a lifetime's pilgrimage. The painting showed Edward looking back one last time.

First-class cricket in England came to an end two months before Edward Hogg's death. It would not return until the summer of 1919. Cricket's re-emergence into the peacetime world was viewed with great trepidation by the game's administrators. To help establish the familiar patterns of the pre-war Golden Age again, a team of Australians toured the UK in 1919. But they were more than a group of talented batsmen, bowlers, fielders and, of course, wicketkeepers.

Each of them had played their part in the great struggle against the wartime foe. Now they would meet English cricketers as former comrades and on-the-field rivals. Crowds flocked to see the 'Colonials' take on the teams that the counties could cobble together from the ravages of war.

My own county, Gloucestershire, met the AIF XI at Clifton College, Bristol and nearly pulled off a famous victory. The Australians' inaugural match took place at Old Buckenham Hall in Norfolk. A couple of years ago I visited this ground to paint a picture recording the return of a handful of those players with the first official Ashes touring team in 1921.

It is over 40 years since the story of the AIF XI has appeared in book form. Since then the internet has opened up access to information that was hitherto impossible to discover.

The untold story of the AIF XI and their tour of Britain, South Africa and Australia in 1919/20 is one of reconstruction. The disastrous Triangular Tournament of 1912 had tempered the enthusiasm for Test cricket, particularly in England.

A total of 275 first-class cricketers were lost in the war, including 12 Test players. At the conclusion of hostilities, despite great enthusiasm in Australia for the resumption of international cricket, the feeling in England was that the county cricket system had to be rebuilt before international cricket could even be considered. However, for the English public, after four years without cricket, there was a thirst for any form of the game.

The excitement that the AIF XI brought to the playing fields of Britain washed away fears that either England or Australia would be too dominant to resume competitive Test cricket, and confirmed to the administrators that public support for international cricket had not waned during the tumultuous years of the war. The competitive nature of the matches and the public support ultimately convinced the MCC that English cricket was ready to resume playing Tests by the Australian summer of 1920/21. Although the 5-0 whitewash the Australians handed the English suggests they had recovered more quickly from the war, the public enthusiasm convinced administrators that the days of the unprofitable pre-war tours were over.

The story of Test cricket is greater than any one team, but there are few teams more important in the story of international cricket than the non-Test-playing Australian Imperial Forces XI.

Jack Russell MBE

Gloucestershire, December 2021.

Acknowledgements

Tim Jones, Worcestershire County Cricket Club Heritage Group

Paul Goodman, Yorkshire County Cricket Club Heritage Manager

Zofia Sulej, Wits Historical Papers Research Archive, University of Witwatersrand, Johannesburg

Robert Curphey and Neil Robertson, Lord's Archives

Roland Burke, Emma Robertson and Charles Fahey – La Trobe University

Thomas Fletcher – Leeds Beckett University

Jack Russell for permission to reproduce 'Cricket at Old Buckenham, Norfolk'.

Additional funding was received from the Department of Archaeology and History, La Trobe University, Melbourne, Australia.

Introduction

THIS IS a story of the first Australian cricketers to tour England following the conclusion of the Great War – the Australian Imperial Forces XI – and the 'fillip' it gave to cricket as it toured Britain, South Africa and Australia in the first domestic seasons after the conflict.

As is the way with stories of sport set in great wider narratives, it would be easy to veer into the world of myth-making and hagiography.

The story of these cricketing Anzacs on what was a real-life propaganda tour, lives up to the mythology of the egalitarian values of the Digger; from abandoning rank to sending home a captain, mateship and the fair go were the bedrock upon which these soldier cricketers rebuilt the foundations of cricket as they toured war-ravaged Britain. This tour sets the mood for the following century of Australian cricketers from

Bradman to Ponting, who all played under the legacy of the AIF XI.

For the English crowds the tour was a chance to look beyond the destruction and shattered lives of the war to a pastime fondly remembered and to a future full of opportunity. Through the metaphor of cricket, this book shows a Britain overcoming the shock of the war to take stock of the cost, and what this should mean for the future.

The format of this book is to introduce each of the players individually, as well as some of their English competitors, while they make their way through their tour of 1919. This is largely chronological. However, it is structured thematically as we visit the cricketing world in post-war Britain.

Before launching into the tour we examine the pre-war problems in cricket up to the wave of cancellations that spread across the cricketing world in the first two years of the war. Next, we look at cricket transitioning from an 'emergency' standing to that of a sport supporting a nation at total war, dedicating what resources – in land, equipment, manpower and motivation – it could to the war effort.

The initial spark for the AIF XI came with Lord Hawke's 1917 proposal for the post-war rebuilding of domestic and international cricket. Through this initial phase we look at the frustrations and anxieties that members of the 'Empire of Cricket' felt about the prospects of a return to cricketing 'life as normal' at the end of the war.

In the early matches of the AIF XI tour, we look at the transition from soldier to sportsman. The first match was a friendly affair glimpsing a fading era with a 'Country House' match against L.G. Robinson's XI at Old Buckenham Hall. Next, we return to old anxieties around funding and ability to see how they manifest now the war was over; would either nation be embarrassed? Would the games be a financial success? Australian victories on the field put at ease doubts about the players' abilities, while their county opponents were victorious at the turnstiles, not just assuaging misgivings about the financial viability of this tour, but those of future tours and the counties themselves.

The first match against a county side in Essex gives us a chance to meet two English sporting heroes, one military and one of the cloth. Johnny Douglas and the Rev. Frank Gillingham represented two sides of British religious and military culture. Following matches against Cambridge University and

Middlesex, a quiet match at Oxford University gives us space to reflect on the centrality of Christian faith in the British and Australian cultures in general, and in the lives of individual cricketers – the survivors of a war that some had been fighting for the best part of five years.

The first significant on-field challenge for the Australians came in the form of matches against Surrey at The Oval, Marylebone Cricket Club (MCC) at Lord's, and Sussex at the County Ground in Hove. These were three of the most influential clubs in the English county game and were central to the rebuilding of the County Championship following the war. However, the first two matches were largely overshadowed by the major crisis of the tour – not one surrounding ability or finances as expected, but around rank and leadership. This was the controversy surrounding the departure of the AIF XI's first skipper, Capt. Charles Kelleway, the only existing Test player on the team. The strict hierarchy of the military – and the establishment that it represented – clashed with the Digger ideals, hard fought on the battlefield, and already established in Australian cricket during the egalitarian player-run Australian tours of recent decades.

The games against the great northern counties of Lancashire and Yorkshire bookend an examination of the intensively competitive Yorkshire and Lancashire cricket leagues. The professional leagues were often controversial. Various high-profile 'cricket mercenaries' not only played during the war, but perhaps more scandalously would play for any team, not just their birth county and country.

After the war many cricket clubs across the empire would have a memorial honouring their fallen team-mates. However, few, and none amongst first-class sides, would share quite as much loss as Hampshire. When the AIF visited the County Ground in Southampton they faced a side ravaged by the war. Hampshire lost more first-class cricketers than all of Australia. Here we pause to reflect on the loss brought by the war.

For the next match against the Gentlemen of England we reflect on amateurism in cricket. Then we journey northwards again, stopping at Northamptonshire, before a tour of Scotland, where we look at some of the more social aspects of a cricket tour in the early 20th century. Then cricket takes a back seat in our tale to other sports when the AIF XI visit Durham and Leicester, as the All-England Tennis Championships were underway at

Wimbledon, the inter-allied sports were taking place in Paris, and the Henley Regatta resumed from its war hiatus.

The cricketing schedule in July in England is a full one, and for the AIF XI it was no different. Following a match against Derbyshire and a friendly against HK Fosters XI, came a whirlwind of five county matches in a row to set the tone of the Australians' summer: three wins and two draws put the question 'could this team match an English XI' on the tips of tongues around the cricketing world. While the pundits speculated, the players took another, more leisurely trip to Scotland in place of a cancelled Irish tour – the reason behind which remained a mystery up until now.

The cricketing season reached its climax in August and September with the great festivals. The AIF make appearances at Canterbury Week, Cheltenham, Clifton Week and Scarborough festivals. We take advantage of this to look at the cricket festival. The festivals peaked with two matches against South of England, and the closest the team sees to an All England side – CI Thornton's XI.

The final match in England was an appropriately friendly match against Mitcham at the Cricket Green.

This was followed by a farewell dinner at Café Monico, where all those with an interest in the tour, the players, administrators, and officers, enjoyed a feast and toasted the success of the side. More than just a fillip to the game, in the words of the Bishop of Taunton: 'The hope that as we became more and more bound together in our Empire that as in cricket we might go forward, and whether in politics, commerce, or in arranging tariffs and preferences we might play the game, and in that way we might join together in one great united Empire.'

The final legs of the tour in South Africa and Australia served the dual purposes of a propaganda vehicle for the AIF, in addition to invigorating cricket wherever they went. Although by now, largely thanks to the AIF XI, the future of cricket was secured. On these two triumphal final legs we will consider the legacy of the AIF XI.

Pre-War Problems: The Triangular Tournament and the Crisis in County Cricket

Prior to the Great War cricket was experiencing three major problems: the first was the loss of faith in the viability of Test cricket following the disastrous Triangular Tournament of 1912 featuring England,

Australia and South Africa in England; second was the accompanying 'Big Six' dispute between Australian players and administrators over control of Australian cricket; and the third was the 'County Cricket Crisis' in England.

Out with the Players, In with the Administrators

The final decade of the 'Golden Age of Cricket' (1890–1912) was dominated by the transfer of power over international cricket away from the players to administrators. Although the Ashes had secured its place as *the* premier cricketing contest, the viability of the tours themselves was in question. Archie MacLaren's side of 1901/02 embarked on the last privately funded English tour of Australia. After losing £1,000 on the 1903/04 tour, MCC, who had taken over organisation of English tours, demanded that future tours of Australia be indemnified by Australian clubs and organisations. In contrast, the privately funded Australian tour of 1905 saw each of the players return home £900 richer.

However, that was the last time the Australian players would pick their own captain, the last tour organised and funded under player control, and the last tour for over 15 years to turn a profit. There had been decades of failed attempts at centralising the control of Australian cricket. These were thwarted mainly by the rivalry between the Melbourne Cricket Club and the New South Wales Cricket Association (NSWCA); neither of the poles of power of Australian cricket were willing to give the other the upper hand. However, while the Australians were playing their opening match of the 1905 tour of England, representatives of the various state boards met and agreed to take all control off the players.

The English tour of Australia in 1907/08 was a financial failure, as too was the 1909 Australian tour of England, although, fortunately for the players, the finances were out of their hands. So while the new administrators counted their losses, the players at least took home some money, albeit less than a third of what they had made on their previous tour. A similar process had taken place in South Africa, with an analogous rivalry between main centres in the 'North' and the 'South' – Cape Town and Transvaal – and between the players and administrators. This saw the administrators in Transvaal take over control of the game.

In 1909 South African diamond magnate and cricket devotee Abe Bailey began pushing for the three

Test-playing nations – England, Australia and South Africa – to play a regular Triangular Tournament. Bailey's suggestion that South Africa host was shot down by Australia, but it was decided the idea was a good one and it was settled that Australia would join South Africa when they were next due to visit England in 1912 and a round robin format tournament would be played. Almost immediately after centralising control at the national level, the administrators had successfully centralised control at an international level under the newly formed Imperial Cricket Conference.

England, under the auspices of MCC, visited Australia in 1911/12, and lost money – even with an indemnity from the Australian boards and a huge crowd of 96,000 at Adelaide that resulted in then record gate takings for a Test match of over £4,000.

However, the tensions between Australian players and administrators now came to a head. The details of what came to be known as 'The Big Six Incident' are for a different book. However, for the purposes of giving us the context of the AIF XI, it is important to understand the strains in Australian cricket at the time. Although most easily understood as a battle between on-field talent and off-field management over control of the game – including in this instance, the selection of the tour manager – this clash also had elements of the interstate power struggle between Victoria, supported by South Australia, and New South Wales, supported by Queensland.

The main catalyst was a disagreement between players and administrators over selection for matches for the 1911/12 Ashes, with Clem Hill arguing for the inclusion of Charlie Macartney instead of Ashley Minnett. Selector Peter McAlister replied that if the third selector, Frank Iredale, agreed with Macartney's inclusion then it should be Hill who made way; an absurd request given Hill's position as the player-elected captain and selector.

When the two were finally in a room together to pick the team for the fourth Test, matters climaxed with the near defenestration of McAlister by Hill from the selection offices. Although Hill would play the fourth and fifth Tests he immediately resigned from the selection committee. The selection for the upcoming Triangular Tournament was already underway, and just a few days after the incident invitations were sent out to players. Hill was not among them. Additionally, the players were advised that they would not be able to pick their own manager; this would be a board responsibility. It was the last straw for the Australian players. Six of the biggest names in Australian cricket: Clem Hill, Warwick Armstrong, Vernon Ransford, Tibby Cotter, Victor Trumper and Hanson Carter all announced they would boycott the tour. Only Carter and Armstrong would ever play Test cricket again. Trumper, one of the all-time greats, died of kidney disease in 1915, Cotter would be Australia's only Test casualty in the Great War, and Hill was 43 by the time the war ended. Vernon Ransford seems to have paid the biggest price for the boycott: although he never played again for Australia, he continued to play for Victoria until 1930, and was considered by some at the time of his retirement 'the best left-handed batsman the state has ever produced'.

The Triangular Tournament

The English summer of 1912 was the wettest since records began in the mid-18th century. Rainfall was double the average, and it was the most miserable August of the entire century. The already weather-depressed crowds barely bothered to attend the Australia v South Africa matches. In 1909 when the plan was devised, the English had recently lost a series in South Africa; the South African spin bowlers had become deadly on the matting wickets used there, especially following the invention of the 'googly'. However, by 1912, bowlers around the world had learnt the delivery, meaning batsmen all over the world had learnt how to play it. This, with a team far less talented than their predecessors, combined to make the South African side an embarrassment as they were trounced in every match.

The Triangular Tournament was so unsuccessful that the immediate response was to cancel any thoughts of future multi-nation tournaments, a policy that held true until the development of one-day cricket.

Abe Bailey's motivation for promoting the Triangular Tournament was about more than cricket. Bailey was an imperialist through and through, and saw the Triangular Tournament as a way of cementing South Africa's place within the empire. This was a turbulent time in South African history; the Second Boer War was a mere decade in the past, and the Union itself was only a few years old. Through the Triangular Tournament, Bailey saw an opportunity to cement his own interests as one and the same as the interests of the South African nation and British Empire.

As a dominion, South Africa did not have control over its foreign policy and therefore could not choose to sit the war out. However, there was considerable tension within South Africa from the Afrikaner population over supporting the British war effort, while the South African Native National Congress – forerunner of the African National Congress – saw support for the war as a negotiating chip in the improvement of civil rights.

It would be far too much to give cricket the central place in binding South Africa to the empire – gold is a far better candidate for that position. However, despite the low crowds and financial losses, the Triangular Tournament still served to strengthen the bonds of empire. We will see this replicated on the AIF XI's return voyage.

County Cricket Crisis

The second major problem facing cricket at the outbreak of the war was what was reported at the time as the County Cricket Crisis. *Leicester Daily Post* sport correspondent, Alfred Gibson, wrote in 1913 that only three counties were in 'satisfactory financial positions': Yorkshire, despite losing £1,000 the previous year, had solid asset and membership bases; Surrey, although they had just delayed scheduled upgrades; and Kent, the only county actually making enough money to service their debts. Other counties, such as Derbyshire and Leicestershire, were seeing increases in their revenues, but off low bases, or while carrying large levels of debt.

This led to a situation in 1913 where several of the larger counties, notably Lancashire, sought to reduce the number of first-class counties by five. This was in order to reduce the financial load on running a county side, as it would require less travel and should result in better attendances. Additionally, Northamptonshire – one of the five slated to go – had a counter-proposal to reduce the playing days from three to two, while increasing the hours of play each day. Ultimately, none of this could be agreed upon, and the suggestions were withdrawn 'Until after the season of 1917'.

Thus the field was set for the county season of 1914 to get underway without controversy. As *Cover-Point* wrote in May in the *Sheffield Daily Independent*:

> The raging, tearing propaganda which a year ago was crying out for a revolution in the game has subsided and peace happily reigns.

> It was the fine weather of the summer of 1913 that did it. If we can only have another summer as fine this year the cranks who have busied themselves in propounding fantastical schemes, which are certainly 'not cricket', will find their occupation gone.

How *Cover-Point* must have considered those words just a few months later.

The Great War

> Whatever happens, Australia is part of the Empire right to the full. Remember that when the Empire is at war, so is Australia at war. That being so, you will see how grave is the situation.
>
> So far as the defences go here and now in Australia, I want to make it quite clear that all our resources in Australia are in the Empire and for the Empire and for the preservation and security of the Empire.
>
> Prime Minister Joseph Cook, Horsham, Victoria, 1 August 1914

Australia's response to the outbreak of war in Europe in August of 1914 was immediate. The full resources of the nation would be mobilised to fight for the mother country. What artist Arthur Streeton called the 'absolute flower of Australia' combined with their trans-Tasman brethren, and the Anzacs set sail to battlefields on the other side of the planet.

In England, MCC president Lord Hawke proclaimed: 'We shall carry on.' There was no need to cancel the County Championship that year: 'Implicit faith in our Navy allays unnecessary fears; so far, there is no immediate danger. To cancel cricket fixtures appears to be altogether unreasonable.' Yet, despite this confidence that the war would remain distant, there was an acknowledgement that all cricketers were expected to do their duty – either on the Western Front or Home Front. However, reality soon overtook cricket – men enlisted, fields were requisitioned, and the idea of playing a game while your chums were playing *the* game was becoming untenable.

There has probably never been a more authoritative 'voice of cricket' than WG Grace in the early 20th century. So it is not surprising that it was he who settled the matter with a short letter to *The Sportsman* on 27 August:

The County Championship limped and lurched to a definitive, if unsatisfactory, conclusion, and the Scarborough Festival for that year was abandoned. When they would reappear five years later the draw card would be a group of Australians, at the end of what for some was a five-year tour. However, the professional Lancashire League would continue with a much-truncated format, while somewhat controversially the Bradford League not only continued as normal but took on professionals from the Lancashire League as they had abandoned the use of players for the duration of the war.

The first impact on Australian cricket came in September, when South Africa cancelled their upcoming tour for financial reasons, as well as the concern over the appearance of impropriety or frivolity. Although indicative of the common belief surrounding the duration of the war, the South African Cricket Association suggested 'the whole Imperial cricket programme [be] put back one year'. The Sheffield Shield season was to go ahead, but over the winter first New South Wales, then Victoria, and finally South Australia withdrew from interstate cricket for the following season. NSWCA president and Australian Board of Control of International Cricket (ABC) secretary Sydney Smith went so far as to refuse to allow interstate fundraising matches for 'patriotic purposes', stating 'it was the associations' duty to assist recruiting in every possible way'.

Local matches would continue – in Australia the focus shifted to club level, in England the attention was on the leagues, friendly and charity matches, and the public schools. After initially choosing to suspend *Wisden*'s annual 'Cricketers of the Year', with no award given in 1916 and 1917 (for the 1915 and 1916 seasons), for 1918 and 1919 the five places were occupied by schoolboy cricketers. Ignoring league cricketers for this award was a not-so-subtle dig at those who chose to play for pay during the war.

Lord Hawke's 1917 Proposal

The second half of 1916 was dominated by the Battle of the Somme. Field Marshal Haig, who believed at the beginning of the year that the Somme would lead to the end of the war, was still resolute that the battle had been a success. However, with close to half a million British casualties it was much harder to sell that success to the people at home. The feeling in the corridors of Lord's among the MCC was one of stout resoluteness as the realisation sunk in that the war was to continue for the foreseeable future.[1] This played out literally on the cricket field – as the verdant sward of the pitch, already transformed into muster grounds, transformed once again into vegetable patches.

But that did not stop some of the old men of English cricket keeping an eye on the future. They looked to a time when the war would end, and cricket could take up its place as the appropriate adjudicator of international battles. Lord Hawke, as the president of Yorkshire County Cricket Club (YCCC) and the president of MCC – the powerhouses of the north and south of England – was perhaps the most influential man in cricket at the time. He first turned his attention to the future of cricket in January 1917.

Addressing the annual meeting of Yorkshire CCC on 31 January 1917, Lord Hawke expressed optimism

---

1 For example, in the minutes of the meetings around this time there is a switch from providing emergency assistance for the army to settling into more permanent arrangements. Properties were more fully turned over to military use, more of the grounds were dug up for vegetable growing, and as put by Lord Harris in a memorandum from the treasurer on 3 February 1917, an institution such as Lord's 'cannot with quietude of conscience stand back in this crisis'.

for the future of cricket after the war. He stated that although there would be some challenges, and changes were required, it would also be a time for improvements. Hawke was thinking about the problems that faced cricket at the start of the war. 'The revival of cricket after the war would have its difficulties. Some things would have to be altered, some concessions made, and in all probability some improvements effected.' It was during this address that Hawke first suggested a change to the Test schedule – England was due to send a team to Australia, but Hawke hoped Australia would send a team to provide 'the necessary fillip to set cricket going again'. This would become the catch cry for the AIF XI tour.[2]

The Jack C. Davis Endorsement

Jack C. Davis wrote cricket stories under the nom de plume *Not Out* and football stories as *The Cynic.* He was part of the editorial teams at the *Sydney Sunday Times*,

---

2 The word 'fillip' may be strange to modern ears, although it was increasing in popularity in the early 20th century, before peaking just after the Second World War. Originally meaning to flick something with your finger, by the 20th century it meant to boost or stimulate an activity.

The Referee, and *Arrow*. As *Not Out* his writings carried the word of cricket to 'everywhere the English language is read'. It was Davis who first suggested that the side could be a military team, even though Hawke had already pointed out the large number of players who had served. Davis agreed it would be easy to alter arrangements to send a team to England, if that was what the English desired. In *The Referee* in February 1917 Davis wrote:

> A series of matches in England, which might answer the purpose of Lord Hawke, and prepare the way for the greater ones between England and Australia, could be arranged when the war closes, the Australian team to be composed of members of the Expeditionary Forces. Several noted Australian players have won military distinctions in battle, and if such men were in an eleven playing a series of matches for the purpose of giving English cricket a fresh start, it would fire the imagination of the people and give to the national game a grander significance than the ordinary Englishman ever associated with it in the lazy pre-war days.

If Hawke's words were the spark of the AIF XI, Davis's were the breath that fanned the embers to a flame, welding together the ideas that Australian cricket could help to rebuild English cricket, and that through associating the war with the game, it would bring cricket a higher reputation than it previously held. Davis could clearly see not just the financial and sporting benefits of such a team, but also the propaganda value such a tour would have for a sport trying to cement a place in the new world that would come at the war's end.

Davis gave a list of players who would be eligible. This included Gordon Campbell, Eric Barbour and Charles Kelleway, who would have central roles to play as the tour came to fruition, plus a number of other players who were serving.

Many of the early sides suggested by the media would include many of the same players. Davis recommended Campbell to captain, with Barbour and Claude Tozer opening the batting, and Jack Massie, Charlie Macartney and Herbie Collins making up a difficult all-left-handed bowling attack. However, only four of the players Davis suggested – Kelleway, Collins, Cyril Docker and Bill Trenerry, were in the final team. This gives some indication of the difficulties to come in selecting a full-strength Australian side from servicemen.

Davis declared Hawke's word should be considered the word of MCC, and by implication the official word of English cricket, and credited Hawke with the inspiration for the idea of a military team: 'The idea of such a venture owes its birth to the appeal made by Lord Hawke.' Billy Stewart, a soldier-cricketer who was serving in England while writing the 'Cricket Gossip' column in *The Referee* as *Short Stop,* said as the team was being formed in late 1918 he believed the idea was originally Lord Hawke's.

Jack Davis never personally took credit for the idea of the AIF XI. However, the fact is that this is the first printed suggestion of a military team, suggesting that some credit for the idea should go to him. Thus, Davis left the glory of the original idea to Hawke, and also laid in his hands the responsibility. He stated it was up to Hawke to convince the secretary of MCC, FE Lacey, of the idea, but that there 'does not appear to be any insuperable obstacles in the way of its realisation if the war does not last longer than the most pessimistic appear to imagine it will'.

Is Australia Strong Enough to Rebuild English Cricket? The Anxieties Begin

The difficulties of arranging a representative Test side were raised almost immediately. Journalist Alfred Pullin was described by *Wisden* as 'one of the foremost authorities on cricket and football in English journalism'. Writing under the pseudonym *Old Ebor* in the *Yorkshire Evening Post*, he wrote that a representative English side could not be put together until county cricket was 'thoroughly re-organised'. He noted that although Australia would have a similar problem, the greater concentration of cricket in Australia, centred on just a handful of cities, would make it easier for the Australians to rebuild.

Lord Harris, newly elected MCC treasurer, and president of the Cricketers' Fund Friendly Society, concurred.[3] Speaking at a meeting of the Cricketers' Fund in July he more fully expressed the problems facing English cricket, following what he assumed was an imminent victory in the war. Harris believed that due to the loss of men during the war, there would be

3 The Cricketer's Fund Friendly Society was a mutual benefits fund set up in the 19th century to help provide for professional cricketers in retirement.

not only fewer players available, but those who were available would need to work more, further restricting their ability to play cricket. In addition, there would be fewer spectators. This meant that when first-class cricket did resume, it would be at a lower volume.

However, the *Star Green 'Un* dismissed the idea that military losses meant the side could not be representative, as although the teams would be depleted '[w]e should know the reason, and be proud of the way the missing heroes have played their part in the greater game'. Although at this stage this was not yet a conversation about the strength and representative nature of a military side versus a true national Test side, this discussion regarding the relative strengths of the teams and whether or not Test status for them was appropriate would continue almost up until the beginning of the tour.

What the cricketing establishment in England could agree on was that Australian strength could be harnessed for the benefit of English cricket. If the strengths of the sides was the great pessimistic talking point of the two years leading up to the start of the tour, the great optimistic talking point was the benefit the tour could have for English cricket. In conversation with Lord Hawke at the end of March 1917, Pullin discussed the benefits of an Australian tour, writing '[h]ence it looks as if the Colonials will have to come to the assistance of the Motherland, in cricket just as they are doing in the fateful days of war'. Although money was rarely discussed there was always the implicit understanding: Australian tours usually brought in a lot of money to the counties, and therefore an Australian tour at the end of the war would be very helpful in getting the counties financially solvent again after the lean years of the war. The *Star Green 'Un* echoed these sentiments, stating that an Australian tour would be 'just the sort of tonic which first-class cricket will be sadly in need of'.

The idea was supported by another of the English cricketing establishment's giants, PF 'Plum' Warner, who would become one of the driving forces behind the tour. Speaking to the London Cricket Conference in early March 1917, Warner positioned the potential tour as important to Australian interests, because 'if the game did not flourish in England cricket in Australia would also be affected' as 'the success of cricket in Australia really depends upon the success of cricket in England, and the visit of an English team is everything to Australian cricket'.[4] Rebuilding England to rebuild Australia would become a common refrain in the years to come. Warner did not seem daunted by the prospect of a representative game as 'the fortunes of war had favoured neither side', instead preferring to speculate on the 'young men unknown to fame' who would fill the spots of the fallen.

Interestingly, in his published response to Warner's words, Davis seemed to have gone cold on the idea of representative cricket as 'the new men of Australia have, Mr Warner, not had any chance of coming on in first-class cricket since the war took hold of the world'. However, a week later, after having spoken to Clem Hill and Warwick Armstrong, along with some 'old cricketers', Davis was more open to the idea of a representative team being sent, for such an opinion was now 'considered … general in this country'.[5] He felt a strong side was

---

4 The London Cricket Conference was the organisation set up during the war to administer cricket among the London clubs and military sides.

5 Armstrong and Hill were two of the 'Big Six' players who had boycotted the 1912 tour, who both supported the idea of a touring side (and had declared themselves fit for it). Notably, neither of the two had served, which shows the state of flux surrounding eligibility in the early days of the tour idea.

possible, as one could 'be certain that every man eligible for inclusion in such a side would consider it his duty to become a member of it'; a prediction that turned out to be quite wrong. It was also Jack Davis who first brought the idea up with Sydney Smith, secretary of the ABC, who gave the idea his 'heartiest support' as in cricket and 'in greater spheres of national life', Australia owes 'everything to the motherland'.

The annual general meeting of MCC was held at Lord's on 2 May 1917, just a month after the entry of the United States into the war which heightened expectations of a swift conclusion. Regarding the proposed Test tour schedule, Lord Hawke suggested that given there were 'so many famous Australian cricketers now on service, rather than sending a team to Australia, those Australians now on active service might stay behind to play in England'. There is no hint here that Hawke was aware of Davis's suggestion but given that several months had passed between the two events, and the interconnectedness of the elite in the global cricketing community, it is likely that Hawke had come across Davis's idea. It is interesting to note that Hawke was speaking of the practicalities of selecting serving military men over a representative team, as they are the ones currently in Europe. This is different to later suggestions that men who have served but already returned home may return to England for the tour. Although a representative side had been widely reported in the media, this suggestion does not appear in either the rough or revised drafts of the minutes for the meeting. This is possibly because, as suggested by the *Yorkshire Post and Leeds Intelligencer*, nothing official can be spoken about while the 'future is so uncertain'.

England v The Dominions

Regardless of the uncertainty of the future, the future must continue to be planned for, and further justification for an all-military team came in July 1917, when international cricket finally returned to Lord's. In a series of matches in the summers of 1917 and 1918, players from across the Western Front could apply directly to Lt. Gen. Birdwood – then in command of Australian troops in France – for leave to return to England to play in charity cricket matches, which was invariably granted if they could be spared.

The morale-building nature of these matches was obvious, as Macartney wrote later: '[i]f cricket could be played in London by men just over from France to participate in a game and return there, then the situation could not be so bad'. Macartney wrote of 'lorry-hopping' from the front to the coast to get on a ship to England, because it was faster than the trains. He wrote of one journey, where he left the front line at 6:30am, hitching rides on the back of motorcycles and in goods trucks until he got to the coast near Boulogne.

Reaching the coast by 2pm, he decided to skip the 2:45pm boat across the Channel to accept a lunch invitation. Even with this delay he was on the 4:45 boat to Folkestone, landing at 6pm, and was in London by 10pm. It is often easy to think of the front as a long way from England, but this example really highlights the proximity of the war. The closeness of the front was also highlighted in another Macartney anecdote. The Army XI v Australian Imperial Forces match in July 1917 was played just a week after 28 German aeroplanes had terrorised London. During the match, planes could be seen flying low and approaching the ground. 'As the day was rather misty, and with a vivid recollection of the previous Saturday, some of the spectators made ready to shelter somewhere, but at the sight of red, white and blue circle on the wings of the planes 'they resumed their seats amidst laughter'.

Army XI v Australian Imperial Forces

The first of what would become a series of charity internationals was held between the English Army XI and Australian Imperial Forces at Lord's to aid the St Dunstan's Hostel for Blinded Soldiers. Would an embattled English populace embrace cricket in the midst of war? As a columnist for *The Globe* wrote: 'For once I didn't care who I saw batting. When an Australian wicket fell I couldn't even get the old thrill of delight. What has happened on the field of battle has settled my cricket partisanship – at least, for a time.' This was supplemented by the strong crowd of 6,000 who showed up to spectate. In Australia the game was followed with 'Unabated interest as though the Ashes were at stake'.

Although far from nationally representative, the match featured seven players with at least one Test cap: Englishmen JWHT Douglas, PF Warner, Neville Knox and Colin Blythe playing his last match of cricket, and Australians Charles Kelleway, Charlie Macartney and Jimmy Matthews. However, to highlight the quality of the English side, only two players would end their careers without playing a Test match. The wicketkeeper Walter Franklin, always beaten to the Test side by professionals, was nonetheless considered the best amateur keeper of his generation. Likewise, David Jennings had had two great seasons for Kent in the lead-up to the war and probably would have earnt a Test cap if he had not succumbed to war injuries in August 1918.

Australia were captained by Eric Barbour, who would go on to select the AIF XI. Barbour had been selected for the aborted tour of South Africa of 1914. However, he would never be picked for Australia again. Docker and Stirling were to join the AIF XI but would never play Tests. However, concerns that the players were not ready for international cricket were confirmed by a slow game exhibiting extreme caution and lack of practice on behalf of the players. Although technically a draw, both sides played a full innings each, on the result of which the English Army were victorious by 31 runs. If not nationally representative, the teams were considered by some to be 'representative of the English Army and Australian Forces', although some felt a better name was 'almost an Australian XI'. The difficulty was that many potential inclusions were on active service in France, Palestine, Salonika and Mesopotamia. It was felt – correctly as it would turn out – that a team put together from all Australians serving in Europe and the Middle East would be much more competitive.

Australia v Indian Gymkhana

Subcontinental cricketers – mostly sons of the nobility or wealthy merchant classes – had been making their way to England for school and cricket for decades. Over the course of the war, over one million troops from the Indian Army would serve outside India. In London, the Indian Gymkhana was formed in 1916 to field a cricket team of players from the subcontinent. Their first match was against an Australian military team, where batsman MP Bajana, founder of the Indian Gymkhana, scored a century, and bowler Churchill Gunasekara took a hat-trick.

When the two sides met again in 1917, a much stronger Australian side had the run of things, and were well ahead when the game finished in a draw. There were several notable players in the 1917 Gymkhana side: after the war Gunasekara would captain Ceylon. He and Bajana were regular players in the county season, for Middlesex and Somerset respectively. KS Pratapsinhji was the nephew of the great Ranji; Paikiasothy Saravanamuttu would go on to be the founding president of the Tamil Union Cricket and Athletic Club, and after whom the Test ground in Colombo, Sri Lanka, is named; Paramasiva Subbarayan went on to be a leader in Indian independence as part of the Quit India Movement, and president of the Board of Control for Cricket in India; John Kotelawala would become prime minister of Ceylon. Batting at No.11 for the Indian Gymkhana was Sir Rantanji Tata, the recently knighted Indian philanthropist and son of the founder of the Tata group of companies. Although representing some of the best of subcontinental cricket, this was more a function of the localised and elite nature of cricket in South Asia at the time.[6] A better description of the side comes from the *Acton Gazette*: 'The Indians are gentlemen who are visiting England to pursue studies for the law, medicine, and other professions.'[7]

English Army and Navy v The Dominions

For the next big charity match the English Navy joined the Army side, and South Africa joined the Australians

---

6 The lack of 'forces' in the Indian Gymkhana match is evidence this is not considered a military game, but it was nonetheless organised by Warner along with the two other games.

7 The 1917 Indian Gymkhana team would make for an interesting examination of the future social and cultural impact of a team of cricketers.

to form The Dominions.[8] PF Warner was again the driving force behind the match, organised for Lady Lansdowne's Officers' Families' Fund, and it had the full approval and support of the Lord's committee. The teams were stronger than the previous match. The English side featured no fewer than eight county players, while for The Dominions side the Test players who played in the previous game were joined by future Test star Johnny Taylor, and Jack Massie, son of former Test captain Hugh Massie. The younger Massie had been selected for the 1912 side for the Triangular Tournament but had been forbidden to attend by his father. In a game against a schoolboy side while playing for Australian HQ just a few weeks before, Jack had taken 7-24 and was thought to be the 'genuine article' by those spectating. This was despite having been shot in the lung and bowling shoulder at Gallipoli – injuries that would keep him out of the AIF XI. The story goes that he had tied a red rag on his non-bowling arm to encourage his opponents to aim there, but the Turkish soldiers had not complied.

---

8 Technically on the scorecard it was 'Australian and South African Forces', but nearly all administrators and media referred to the side as 'The Dominions'.

Even though he looked to be back to form, the injury had already ended his sporting career.

South Africa's star player of the 1912 Triangular Tournament, Sid Pegler, was promoted before the match as leading a South African contingent of four in the side, but he, and two others, did not play in the match. The only South African to play was W. Bell, who does not bother the cricketing records beyond this match, despite making the second highest score. This time The Dominions side were victorious, thanks largely to an Eric Barbour century.

Although this series of matches was described in some papers as 'military Test' matches, it was approved by military officials, not cricket administrators. The *Leeds Mercury* included quotation marks: military 'Test'. This suggests that this was said with an appreciation that it was not a real Test match, more a taste of international cricket for a starved audience.

Within a few weeks the cricket season made way for the football season in the UK, so the focus on international cricket switched to the Australian media, serving a public hungry for cricket season news. But this was a fraught time for the progress of the war. In the second half of 1917 the belligerents were engaged in the

Third Battle of Ypres. The Allies were holding out for the Americans to arrive in full force. Understandably, cricket news was somewhat subdued during this time. However, in the meeting rooms of the ABC a careful optimism was on the rise. At their annual general meeting in late October the board passed the following resolution: 'That in the event of the war terminating within the next 12 months, the Chairman and the Honorary Secretary be empowered, if they deem it necessary, to at once call a special meeting of the board to deal with any matters affecting international cricket.' The ABC wanted to be ready to snap into action at the first possibility of resuming international cricket.

As the summer rolled on in Australia, so too did the Allied war machine.

1918

1918 was only a few days old before Jack Davis again raised the prospect of a military game after the war, writing in *The Referee* on the 2 January:

> The military matches between Australia and England in London aroused tremendous interest ... I think that as soon as peace

> is declared cricket may be set going again by an AIF XI touring England under the management of the Board of Control and the MCC. Prominent English cricketers are of the opinion that such a team would be a tremendous draw. The AIF could, barring the misfortune of war, put a side into the field that would hold its own with England's best. I am certain that if such a trip can be arranged it will be entirely successful. I am equally certain that an Australian team containing eligible men who have not enlisted would not be a success here until some years have elapsed. The feeling is very strong against slackers. There is no IWW element here to cheer them on … I am sure the idea of a team drawn from the Australian military playing in England will be warmly taken up by the MCC if the suggestion is made by Australia.

Again, we see Davis returning to the themes of rebuilding English cricket, and concerns surrounding the potential quality of the sides. The idea that an AIF team would be a big draw card was speaking to the crisis in county cricket already outlined, especially the precarious financial position of many of the counties. Davis had apparently put aside his prior apprehensions on quality and was now confident that a genuinely representative Australian team could be drawn. This article also advised that 'slackers' would not be welcome. This was an important discussion within Australia at the time, coming just two weeks after the failed second conscription referendum; the social trade-off for the freedom of a volunteer army being the shaming of those who did not 'do their duty'.

It is not surprising to see this ambivalence towards those who did not volunteer reinforced here, especially with the reference to the IWW (the International Workers of the World was one of the fiercest voices against conscription in Australia). Finally, Davis notes there would be a warm reception *if the suggestion is made by Australia*, suggesting a possible beginning for the confusion surrounding the organisation of the tour that would come up in late 1918.

However, beyond this article by Davis the talk of post-war international cricket was rather muted until March, when the various committees, clubs, and councils in the UK began having their pre-season meetings. By this time the 'reconstruction of sport after the war [was] in the air'.

England v Dominions

In Australia in March *The Land* reported on talk in the 'Old Country' of a military team. Jack Davis was now convinced that the first post-war Australian tour would be a military one, and supported the idea that a team which included those who did not serve would be rejected by the English public. This stance was made easier now he was convinced a team made up of those currently serving would be able to hold their own. Meanwhile, at a committee meeting at Lord's, Warner moved a motion requesting 'a grant of £50 be made for each of the two charity matches to be organised by him in 1918'. The motion was passed, and it was decided both contests should be military matches titled *England v. Dominions*. However, again, with the sole exception of a mention that the idea of a military game should be played following the war had been well received in England, there was little more mentioned about the future of international cricket, with most of the focus in England on the reconstruction of the county competition.

However, as the games drew closer the excitement levels at the prospect of a resumption of international cricket grew. Around 12,000 were present at the first match, where the Dominions were victorious.

Adding to the strength of the 1917 Dominions team were Roy Park, Johnny Taylor and Johnny Moyes, all of whom were selected in Test sides, although Moyes's 1914 selection was dashed by the war. Also joining the side for the first time was Ed Long, who would be a part of the AIF XI.

Even without Douglas, Knox and Blythe – either now retired or unavailable – the English also fielded a stronger side than they had in 1917. Humphreys, although never a Test player, had over 300 first-class matches to his name. Future Test player Wally Hardinge had been a 1915 *Wisden* Cricketer of the Year. Greville Stevens was a future Test player and 1918 *Wisden* Cricketer of the Year (one of the schoolboy years). The evergreen Colin McIver would represent Essex into his 50s. Kirk, Horsley and Franklin were all County Championship stalwarts, as was the Rev. Frank Gillingham.[9] Plum Warner was already a legend,

---

9 Gillingham was also the first ball-by-ball cricket commentator.

but this match saw a true passing of the torch as the pre-war great CB Fry was (briefly) joined at the crease by Patsy Hendren, who had yet to play for England, but would do so over 50 times. Hindsight is of course a wonderful thing – Hendren already had half a dozen first-class seasons behind him, but was still just a youngster with potential, although his duck in his sole innings was not the best omen for his future success. The Dominions were in the better position when the game ended in a draw.

King George V arrived in full military uniform during the second match a fortnight later, driving around the ground filled with 6,000 spectators, above which flew the Union Jack and the Australian ensign. The king was met by various dignitaries including Lord Hawke, Walter Long (Secretary of State for the Colonies), Lord Harris and FE Lacey. However, rather than going straight to his box, the King walked on to the ground, necessitating a suspension in play. The captain of the Dominions side, Eric Barbour, was then presented to the King. He then met with Warner, the English captain, and watched about 30 minutes of play before leaving. The most notable inclusion for this match was George Gunn, 1914 *Wisden* Cricketer of the

Year, and a Test cricketer at the peak of his powers. The match ended in a draw as rain before the second innings caused the Dominions batsmen to struggle on the proverbial sticky wicket to a score of 34/8 chasing 157 when stumps were drawn. The strong English response helped to allay some of the fears surrounding the quality of English cricket.

There was a third England v Dominions match held on the bank holiday weekend in August at The Oval. The August bank holiday at The Oval traditionally saw a match between Surrey and Nottinghamshire and was a major cricket weekend of the season. Once again there was a strong crowd of over 11,000 leading the *Sportsman* to write it 'was quite like pre-war times'. In this side were three South Africans joining the Australian contingent including Herbie Taylor, who had toured in 1912 and would become a future captain of South Africa. Strengthening the English side was the inclusion of two Test greats who hitherto had not played in the season's charity matches: Frank Woolley and Jack Hobbs.

Interestingly, Hobbs's lack of inclusion up to this point was probably due to an investigation conducted by Warner in May into 'facts regarding the Munition and Military Service of J.B. Hobbs during the present war'. Warner then sought to exclude 'a certain player' (assumed to be Hobbs) from the charity matches at Lord's. Additionally, at least one player for England, Percy Fender (who played a match-saving innings) had already been discharged from the military. Warner had sought approval from MCC to organise the first two, but there is no mention of the third match in the remaining Lord's archives, although it was apparently organised by the Surrey club.

The idea of an AIF team was not just being kicked around in boardrooms and newsrooms. After the second Dominions match, several Australian players approached Warner directly with the suggestion of staying behind after the war to play some matches. The large crowds boded well for the future of international cricket, as noted by Jack Davis:

> The size of the attendance at this match may be regarded as an indication that when the war closes, cricket in England will be well supported by the public, especially if, as suggested, a team of Australian military cricketers who have figured in the war, tour

> the Old Land officially under the Board of Control on this side and the MCC on the other. The board, I am led to believe, will heartily endorse such a proposal if it be mooted from England.

Once again Davis was a driving force behind the idea of an AIF XI, promoting, with a great deal of justification, his idea as one that was generally accepted. However, why Davis now suggested the offer must come from England, in direct contrast to his article in November is unclear. It almost seems as if everyone involved in cricket wanted the tour to happen, but no one wants to be on the hook for it if it did not work. The shy bachelor and coquettish maiden, with Davis the matchmaker. As we will see when the tour moves from idea to planning, this confusion intensifies over who should approach whom, who pays, and even which national organisation should be responsible for the tour.

So it now seemed that MCC was waiting for an approach from the ABC *and* that the ABC was waiting for an approach from MCC. It should have been clear by now that there would be great public support for post-war international cricket and that a tour would likely be very profitable. However, it is quite understandable that after four years of war the psychological toll would be so great that optimism for the future would be muted.

Regardless of the confusion, by this stage the AIF XI was almost a *fait accompli*. The twin themes of an Australian team touring England to help revive cricket, and that said team should be made up of men who served, as this was what the English public would accept, were now being reported as obvious, and that 'the re-establishment of big cricket will be arranged without delay upon the final cessation of fighting seems to be fully understood'.

Australia's Responsibility to the Motherland

From the outset, the war was presented in Australia as an existential threat not only to England, but by extension, the British Empire. A fundraising plea published in *The Farmer and Settler* on 25 August 1914 wrote: 'The war now raging will decide whether Australia shall be British or not, and whether the British Empire shall tumble to pieces or rise to greater power and glory.' Speaking in front of a crowd of supporters in Sydney upon returning home from a tour of the empire in 1916, Prime Minister Billy Hughes proclaimed '[w]e are part and parcel of the empire, but we fight not for Britain, but for ourselves'. This is exemplary of the opinion that even if Australia were its own nation, its first duty was to the Empire, and the first duty of the empire was to protect the mother country. Ergo, the most patriotic Australian duty aligns perfectly with the needs of Britain. Of Hughes, one supportive letter writer to the *Bendigo Independent* in 1917 stated that 'he has the courage to do his duty to the Empire and to Australia, and to those who are now fighting to maintain Australia's honour'.

Fighting a war on the other side of the world that posed no immediate threat to Australian territorial sovereignty was seen as a duty to the king and the empire, as well as to the nation, whose ultimate duty was also to the king and empire. Likewise, this sentiment was used to promote the idea that even though it was rightfully England's turn to tour Australia, it was Australia's duty to tour England. Controversial former Test player and journalist John Worrall cited MCC's 'prescience' at organising the tour, as '[i]t is only proper that while we helped the motherland in the greater game, we should also help to revive interest in the grand and glorious national summer pastime'.[10] Billy Stewart considered it 'a great tribute to Australia to have the honour of rehabilitating the game in the home and Mecca of cricket'.

This 'honour' was perhaps best summed up with a quote from Sam Michael, former first-class cricketer and VFL footballer writing under the name *Onlooker* in *The Referee.* Michael opined that the role of the tour was to 'replenish the coffers of the county clubs, to aid the organisations which of necessity must continue for many years to succour the widows and children of the fallen, [and] to ameliorate the lot of maimed and blind soldiers'.

---

10 John Worrall had many controversies during his lifetime. For example, while on tour with Australia in 1902 he told English umpires that they should be calling his team-mates JV Saunders and MA Noble for chucking. Whilst coach of the Carlton Football Club he instituted a strict training regime that included a ban on drinking. In 1904 he survived a move to unseat him as secretary of Carlton when he was accused of mishandling finances. In 1909 he resigned after players demanded a pay increase. To quote the Australian Dictionary of Biography, he was 'passionately fond of sport without the sideshows' and 'did not make friends easily'.

Happy Christmas (War is Over), it's Time for Cricket

Although by late 1918 victory had been expected for some time, the collapse of the Central Powers was rapid. Between 29 September with the surrender of Bulgaria and the surrender of Austria-Hungary on 3 November, Germany was left without any military allies. Thus, even though the news of the armistice did not reach Australia until 13 November, when the ABC met for its annual general meeting in Sydney on 12 November, the imminent end of the war was palpable. The board passed three motions: one declaring 'thankfulness and pride in the glorious triumph achieved by the Empire and her Allies', a second expressing admiration for cricketers who had 'nobly responded to the call of empire', and a third stating that the 'board takes the earliest opportunity of arranging for the resumption of international cricket'. ABC president Joseph Allen stated that he believed there were enough 'crack players' in England to field a strong team, with only a few additions from those in Australia. It was decided to approach MCC and ask for their advice.

Just a few hours later on the other side of the world MCC met and it was decided to approach the ABC and ask if they would favour sending a services side in 1919.[11] By the time the NSWCA met on Monday 18 November, the request for a side comprised of 'men who had served' had been received and a special meeting to consider the request was called for 6 December. Before the ABC could meet, Jack Davis published another article full of suggestions. It is worth highlighting these suggestions here to compare them to what actually happens to show the influence Jack Davis had in Australian cricketing circles.

Davis had the front page of *The Referee* on Wednesday, 20 November 1918. He stated it was 'now assured that an Australian Military Eleven will tour England in the coming cricket season' as an invitation had been received that was 'certain to be accepted'. Now the finer details of the tour, such as the appointment of administrative personnel like representatives, selectors, managers and scorers, could be speculated on. For example, although the board's previous representative in England, Mr W. Findlay, was available, Davis felt it was

---

11 Interestingly, the MCC did not share this with the media, leading to a complaint in the *Sheffield Independent* that news of the MCC's invite came from 'down under'.

more appropriate that one of the military cricketers be appointed to arrange the tour. To which he recommended Maj. Gordon Campbell, who not only was capable of representing the board's interests and managing the tour but was also a handy wicketkeeper. Davis suggested the selectors should be Campbell, Maj. EP Barbour and Lt. C. Kelleway. He also stated that '[i]t will, no doubt be determined if necessary to despatch any player or players of ability who have seen service and returned to Australia'. However, the logistics of sending players back to England would become a significant sticking point later in the organisation of the tour.

Soldier Cricketers and the Quality of the Side

The second assumption moving into the northern winter of 1918/19 was that the team would be made up of soldiers. Sam Michael believed 'few would be out of sympathy with the suggestion [that the team] should be comprised solely of soldier cricketers' and that any other team 'would have been directly opposed to the sentiment of British-speaking peoples' who 'would decline to attend representative games in which other than military cricketers figured'. However, this view was not universal. An unknown author, writing under the pseudonym *Slips* in *Sporting Judge* brought up the case of Richmond captain Archie Dean, who tried to enlist several times in the army, but had been rejected on each occasion. Dean had actually given up cricket for most of the war, but had just resumed playing with considerable success. The consternation surrounding whether or not the team would be made up of just soldiers was not just about whether or not the public would support a non-military team, or the logistics of fielding a non-military side. It was largely about both English and Australian insecurities over putting together a substandard side.

The *Hull Daily Mail* in May of 1917 responded to Lord Hawke's initial call, stating that the games cannot be considered Test matches, as 'such a team would not, of course, be representative of Australia'. In late 1918, just as FE Lacey had been dispatched by MCC to organise the county season which would include matches by the AIF XI against all the counties, Alfred Pullin reminded his readers that the idea of an AIF XI had been around since the early days of the war and had in the past been considered favourably by both sides. He was of the opinion that there had been enough talent shown in the recent military matches to suggest representative sides would be possible, especially if a few Australians could be sent over to bolster the AIF side. Davis makes the point that due to the actions of the leading associations keeping cricket going it will now be easy to resume and that a 'tolerably good side' could be made out of men in Europe to form an AIF team that would be a 'splendid advertisement' for the game in England.

In other sections of the English press there was a sense that the AIF side would not be up to Test standard, but still 'a reasonably strong side of a semi-representative nature' that 'would not be easy to defeat by the majority of our country sides'. Some in Australia were confident a 'fairly representative team' could be put together. meanwhile, others were straight out referring to it as Test cricket, including a mention of the tour as the 'Ashes'. More common was the opinion of the *Old Cricketer*, reprinted in the *Daily News* in Perth, who was confident that a strong side could be selected, and that for the county games there should be no service qualification for selection in the county side. However, 'in choosing the English team, only men would be included who had done similar war service to that rendered by the selected Australians'.

For this reason 'there will be a disposition to regard the England–Australia matches of the tour as other than formal tests' and there 'will be time enough to resume the historic contests, surrounding the custody of the visionary venerated Ashes, when cricketers have fully regained form'. No one would want to see the Ashes won or lost by under-strength teams.[12] For Sam Michael the true representative quality of the sides was 'of secondary importance, since Australia has available so many players of distinction who at the supreme moment offered their lives cheerfully and unflinchingly for the Empire that no difficulty would be experienced in forming a combination to worthily uphold the traditions of Australian cricket', adding that given England had conscription and was on the front line of the war, they had lost so many cricketers a services team would be a more equal competitor.

But for some, even two military teams would be unequal. Writing from Queensland in the *Daily Standard*, in November of 1918 Solomon Gay stated that

---

12 Interestingly, this article by 'Old Cricketer', written on 26 October when mentioning the possibility of cricket starting up in November of the Australian summer of 1918/19, writes 'but we can scarcely dare to hope that the conflict will terminate so soon'. The armistice would be signed just over two weeks later.

while England had lost two of her most 'famous players' in the war, Australia had not lost any international players killed in action.[13] Although the point remains, Gay forgets Tibby Cotter's death in a charge with the 4th Light Horse Brigade against Turkish troops in 1917.

---

13 Solomon Gay began his journalistic career writing poetry in *The Star* (Sydney) in 1910 and following a few other reporting positions around the nation in 1911 and 1912, began sport reporting for the *Daily Standard* (Brisbane) in 1913, a position he held until 1919. It is not known who Gay is referring to here. Colin Blythe had been a stalwart of the English side from 1901 but had not been selected in a Test side since 1910, despite good form. There were two 'active' English Test players killed in the war, both of them *Wisden* Cricketers of the Year – Major Booth (a given name, not a rank) and Kenneth Hutchings. A fourth Test player of little note who had been killed in the war, Leonard Moon, had retired from cricket in 1909. Perhaps most interesting is that it is never considered that South Africa's losses in the war were a significant impediment to their rebuilding of cricket. Yet of the three Test-playing nations, they were the worst hit. Seven South African Test players died in the war. However, most of these had only played a handful of Tests and this is probably more a reflection on the shallow pool of cricketing talent in South Africa, and that both cricket and fighting for England would have drawn on the same relatively small English population in South Africa.

Cotter had been one of the mainstays of the Australian side for more than a decade before the war, and his death was widely covered in both the English and Australian press. His frightening pace had earnt him the nickname 'The Terror' among English fans. Even to this day his strike rate is the 32nd-highest of all time among players who have played at least 20 Tests. This slots him in behind Glenn McGrath and Dennis Lillee. At the time it was the eighth-best strike rate in history. This aligns with the feeling promoted by *The Land* mentioned previously that England had suffered more in the war despite similar casualty lists. But the claim is far more valid in this case. Fifteen Australian first-class cricketers were killed in the war (one Test, 14 Shield). For England, even though only three Test players were killed during the war the number was closer to 200.[14] Although it should be noted that Australia had six first-class sides to more than 30 in England – although many were of dubious quality – including 16 counties, MCC, and Oxford and Cambridge Universities. Added to this were

---

14 One of the three Test players, Major Booth, only went on the one tour of South Africa in 1913/14, hence not being included in Gay's 'famous players'.

representative games like South v North or Gentlemen v Players, and the opportunities for a first-class cap in England were far greater than in Australia. Regardless, the point is rather moot; all cricketing nations suffered losses in the war. Also noteworthy from Gay's article was that he stated that the last touring side was JWHT Douglas's English touring Australia in 1912/13. This is not accurate. Douglas had taken over the captaincy of MCC for an ill PF Warner during the 1911/12 tour of Australia and had been the acting captain for all five Test matches. While not serious mistakes, the neglect of Cotter, and getting wrong easily verifiable dates that should be known by an Australian cricket journalist, raises some questions about his motives.

Aside from whether a soldier team could be considered a Test team, even the suggestion of a military only side was not universally supported. Even once the team was announced there was still scepticism regarding the tour as a soldier-only affair, with some feeling it was better to 'drop the soldier idea, and revert to the old order, getting together the strongest combination that Australia can produce'.

Former Australian Test cricketer and journalist John Worrall expressed concerns with a soldier cricketer side. Firstly, he rejected the idea of only allowing 'eligibles' (men who served) to be selected for the 1918/19 Sheffield Shield competition, stating that if such a rule went ahead there would be 'no representative matches in Melbourne this cricket season'. Regarding the AIF XI, whilst admitting he 'knows nothing of the details', Worrall expressed concerns that 'cricket and war should be things apart'. He stated that unless the side was truly representative then international tours should be left until each nation can get their local competitions back on a firm footing 'before perpetuating any ill-feeling'.

This suggests Worrall was concerned that rather than bringing the countries closer together, as was the popular opinion, an international tour could rouse the antagonistic feelings that had been present in previous tours. Interesting coming from the man who would popularise the phrase 'bodyline' 15 years later. A week following his piece, after the board had met to approve the tour, Worrall listed potential selections and wrote that although 'a fine team can be chosen' it was 'not really representative of the strength of Australian cricket'. However, he had softened his opinion on the antagonistic potential of the tour, stating 'the tour is bound to perform a lasting benefit to the grand old game'.

The opinions of the sporting press as to the quality of the side are important, as there was an apparent anxiety amongst administrators that neither side should be humiliated. This also goes to the question of whether or not to consider the matches Tests, which ultimately decided who paid for the tour.

Financial Anxiety

The representative nature of the side, and therefore, whether the matches would be 'Test' matches, had financial implications that extended beyond the precarious financial situation of the counties. Granting the tour official Test status would put both MCC and the ABC on the hook financially, as the accepted funding model was that the visitors would fund the tour up front, and collect a percentage of the gate money, but that if that was not sufficient to cover all the costs, the host body would indemnify the tourists over a loss. As the AIF XI became more of a reality, the anxiety extended beyond whether or not the tour would be a help or a hindrance in kick-starting the game, but also whether or not it could financially damage the national organisations which had had five lean years due to war.

Plum Warner was certain that the AIF XI 'would undoubtedly "draw", and would help to popularise cricket, and to tide us over the difficult first year'. Warner compared the cost of an AIF team touring England to that of sending an English team to Australia. Sending an English team to Australia, however, would require scouring the country for an entirely new team, along with the extra costs of organising such a tour so quickly. The Australians, on the other hand, were already in England, and if they were to play the full season in England that would serve as the scouting opportunities to find the next generation of English Test players. Warner was one of the optimists, having 'no fear for the future of cricket'. One view in Australia was that the tour's success was assured because of the reputation the soldiers had earnt: 'Owing to the heroism with which the Australians at the front have borne themselves in the war such a tour should be immensely popular.' Sam Michael saw financial advantages in a military team as the cost of sending the team to Europe would be spared, as would that of sending a manager, if, as suggested by Jack Davis, that role went to Gordon Campbell. He also hoped that the railway companies and hotels may give discounts, or that they could stay as guests of officers at barracks.

Added to this was whether or not cricket would be able to survive at all in the post-war world. Before the first series of games were played there was a 'belief that in the upsetting of old customs and traditions as part of the turmoil and aftermath of war the game would never regain the high place it once held in the estimation of Britons; that another sense of proportion had been created, that the serious problems of life would be too absorbing to give cricket, or indeed, any other pastime, it's old eminence'.

A Team of Eligibles

As they had reserved the right to do at the 8 November annual general meeting, the board called an emergency meeting to discuss international cricket in Sydney on 6 December. Although the meeting was not open to the press, the board provided copies of the motions passed. A motion for 'a team of men who have served touring England in 1919' was carried unanimously. A separate motion was moved by Mr H. Gregory, the West Australian delegate, that the team should be made up of men who served overseas as members of the AIF. This was a notable distinction as it excluded men who had enlisted, but not travelled to the front, as well as men who had served at the front as members of NGOs such as the Red Cross or the Australian Comforts Fund.

No reason was given to the press regarding this decision, but it is notable that these organisations were primarily led and staffed by conservative, upper- and middle-class women, but were not pacifist organisations like some other patriotic support groups. This meant the significant exclusions of two players mentioned in several suggested sides that had been printed as the hype around the tour built. South Australian batsman Dr Donald Steele (Red Cross) who was a batting prodigy before enlisting, and Dr Herbert Hordern (Australian Comforts Fund) who before the war was considered the best leg-spinning googly bowler in the world.

The next motion carried was put by Mr Rush that Maj. Campbell and Mr Findlay should represent the board to negotiate with MCC, combining Davis's previous suggestions. But Davis was not all-powerful in either prediction or influence. Although Barbour and Campbell were appointed as selectors as Jack Davis had suggested, rather than having Kelleway as the third selector – following the already well-established Australian norm of having the captain on the selection committee – the board chose Capt. Roy Park. The board also voted that selections would have to be finalised by them and that they would appoint the captain and vice-captain. This is important because it highlights the board's desire to retain control over the team; something that matters both when answering the question of whether the team was representative – a non-representative team would not require such board oversight – and in light of the board's takeover of control that had happened prior to the war. Although selection would remain with Campbell, Barbour and Park, the board presented a list of names who 'had represented Australia in the war'.[15] They were:

New South Wales: EP Barbour; CG Macartney; C. Kelleway; RJ Massie; HR Pratten; C. Docker; Collins; JN Taylor; F. Buckle; CJ Tozer; GC Wilcocks; EJ Long; PW Docker; FC Berry; WJ Stack; NM Cragg; A Diamond

---

15 *Slips* is the only reporter to list the names, although the existence of a list of names is verified by G. Mostyn Evan, the South Australian delegate to the board.

Victoria: RL Park; J. Fitzpatrick; GS Down; C. Willis; W. Sewart; W. Matthews; A. Lampard; G. Johnstone; C. Sandford; AR Errington; E. Cameron; A. Ferguson; Onyons; J. Cusdin; R. Herring; W. Daly

South Australia: GC Campbell; GA Moyes; C. Pellew; W. Stirling; JJ Munday; Dr Steele

Queensland: McAndrew; Sheppard; Maynard

The sheer size of the list is illustrative of the tussle for national power between the states. New South Wales and Victoria dominate this list as they dominated Australian cricket, pushing names seemingly for volume over quality. None of the Queensland suggestions were eventually picked, but it would have been important to the Queenslanders to have representation on the list, particularly in light of an internal battle for control going on in the Queensland Cricket Association.

From the South Australian list Campbell, Pellew and Stirling were all to be involved in the side, and Moyes probably would have been selected if he had not returned home in January 1919. But the South Australians argued for the inclusion of Dr Donald Steele, made ineligible by excluding members of the Red Cross. Additionally, Dr Hordern of the Australian Comforts Fund made the suggested lists of John Worrall, Billy Stewart, and *Slips*, amongst others. Interestingly, the article in the *Advertiser* on 12 December includes HV Hordern, but recognises that he could not be included due to not serving in the AIF, and corrects itself the following day writing: '[t]he Dr Hordern mentioned in the list yesterday is not the HV Hordern who did so well for New South Wales in interstate cricket before the war'. However, it is more likely the paper did mean Dr HV Hordern and had made the same mistake as the other papers in not realising his ineligibility, as there was only one H. Hordern (Herbert Arthur Hordern) enlisted in the AIF in World War One. This H. Hordern was only 20 at the time, and seemingly has no history of cricket documented in either the newspapers or his military service records.

At the meeting Sydney Smith also moved that the name of the team should be 'The AIF Australian Eleven'. This would seem to suggest that the board was not committing to a representative team. However, it was also decided at the meeting to approve the playing of Test matches. But this was likely based on the assumption that a truly representative side, made up of all those who had served, including those who had already returned, or would have returned by the time the tour started, could be selected. As noted in the *Daily Telegraph*, selection of the returned players was a 'certain'. The *Argus* reported that at the meeting it was agreed to inform the selectors in England of eligible men who had returned and that the board would pay their travel expenses back to England. The board suggested four names: the now returned Bill Sewart, AG 'Johnny' Moyes, Bert Pratten and Austin Diamond. This information seems to have been announced by the board at a separate time, as Worrall, writing a week after the meeting, explicitly says '[i]t is not known at the present juncture whether any return cricketers are eligible for selection, or whether they are all to be chosen from overseas. Expense might be considered an item of importance.'[16] However, the article was amended before publication to announce the payment for travel arrangements and names suggested mentioned above. The *Yorkshire Post and Leeds Intelligencer* reported that the telegram was sent to the selectors on 10 December.

---

16 This suggests the acceptance of returned players was a late breaking piece of news.

Selection was to start instantly, for if players from Australia were to make it to England in time for the first match beginning in the first week of May they would have to leave Australia by early March. However, it was noted by the *Daily Telegraph* that it would be 'rather unlikely that many players would be sent from Australia'. If the board were to want to send the possible strongest side then several players would have to make their way back to England.

Davis suggested that 20 men should be chosen to practise for two weeks prior to selection being made as it would allow the selectors to evaluate the physical condition of the men, as well as to determine whether each man had gotten better or worse over the years of the war. Regardless of whether this is Davis's influence, prescience, or common sense, this was what ultimately happened.

Mr H. Gregory was appointed to speak to both the acting Prime Minister William Watt, and Defence Minister George Pearce, to request any AIF member selected be allowed to stay in England and to arrange the necessary leave from service.

Also decided at the meeting was that Campbell would be manager and treasurer, and that WH

Ferguson would be the scorer.[17] Davis wrote that even though Campbell was chosen he would 'no doubt ... desire to return to Australia at the earliest possible time', mentioning a young son whom he had never seen. It was also decided that the tour would be financed through subscriptions based on each state association's representation on the board. Therefore, as of this meeting, which officially accepts the English invitation, the following conditions were set: the side will be called the 'AIF Australian Eleven', it will be a representative Test side under the control of the board, it will be financed by the board through subscriptions from the states, and it will be comprised of men who had served overseas in the AIF. The anxieties surrounding the quality of the team, and whether they would be considered representative, as well as the

---

17 W.H. Ferguson, or 'Fergie' was and is probably the greatest scorer and baggage handler ever involved in Test cricket. He revolutionised scoring, creating the now omnipresent 'wagon wheel', and scored 208 Test matches over 49 years working in and for Australia, New Zealand, England, the West Indies and South Africa. He was the brother-in-law of Australian legend Monty Noble and was taught how to score by Frank Laver. It is likely there is not a more important, yet obscure, figure in world cricket.

question of who would fund the tour, were apparently answered.

In England there was commonality to the facts reported. This was that the invitation had been accepted, the team will be called the 'AIF Australian XI', Campbell had been selected manager, and that returned soldiers could play. The most complete report appears in *Sporting Life* where it was written that an Australian side under the management of Campbell will be arranging fixtures, and that the board had requested an MCC side to tour in 1919/20. The *Nottingham Evening Post* reported on the request for an MCC tour, but suggested that after the rigours of the war, there would not be enough time in the 1919 season to discover the most representative side. It also repeats the rebuttal posed in the *Daily Telegraph* that the Australians were in much the same spot. *The People* noted that the MCC advisory committee meeting to be held on 16 December will decide fixtures, and that the 'Australian military team' will play 'at least one attractive feature at every county ground'. It also expressed concern at the ability to field a representative side to tour Australia in 1919/20, but 'whether the date be next autumn or twelve months thereafter, it is England's turn to send a team out to the Commonwealth'. In addition to publishing the board's acceptance of the tour, along with Campbell's appointment as manager, and the request for an MCC side in 1919/20, *The Field* recounted that at a meeting of the Sussex County Cricket Club it was 'decided cordially to support the proposed matches with the Australians'.

The most interesting aspect here is that there was no mention of the team being a Test side. When combined with the anxiety over whether England would be able to field a team by the end of 1919, it suggests that the plan for the tour to be representative was both not heard of in England, nor would it be agreeable to the English. Indeed, the *Yorkshire Post and Leeds Intelligencer* stated that '1919 is expected to be an Australian season [i.e., Australia will tour in 1919], though not in the Test match sense'. Despite this, the *Advertiser* in Adelaide reported, '[i]t is believed that the All-England teams to meet the AIF eleven will be comprised solely of soldiers'. Unfortunately, there is no indication given as to who believes this, or why the author believes it, as this is the only mention of such an idea.

But across Australia the ink flowed with ebullient enthusiasm for the tour. The *Ballarat Courier* implored that the 'Australian board has no need to delay its approval'. Sam Michael wrote 'immediate acceptance is assured, at least on its vital principle, which would be impossible logically to oppose'. *Old Cricketer* was a little more circumspect, only going so far as to say the proposal was sure to receive 'careful and sympathetic consideration', although he then gives his list of 13 players who should be selected. However, as 1918 moved into 1919 the debates surrounding who would be eligible, the status of the matches, and increasingly, anxiety over the financial arrangements for the tour flared up again and were compounded by the tyranny of distance and an inexplicable gap in communications between Australia and her representatives in England.

1919

1919 began with a meeting of MCC's General Purposes Subcommittee on 2 January. Sydney Smith's telegram response to the MCC invitation was read out:

> Board approves suggested tour, Major Campbell and Major Findlay, Surrey, appointed, negotiate terms, communicated Findlay – Smith.

The 'suggested tour' was referring to the MCC telegram that requested 'an Australian team composed of those serving'. It is notable what was not included in this communication. There was no mention of the makeup of the side, the representative nature (and therefore Test status) of the games, the name of the side, or the financial arrangements agreed to by the board. This was presumably communicated to Findlay by the ABC, although such a record does not exist.

Clearly Test status was agreed upon in a private meeting, the contents of which are now lost.[18] The important thing here is that both the ABC and MCC have agreed that the MCC v AIF XI matches would be official Test matches.[19] The full programme probably refers to following similar tour schedules as previous tours. This was five Tests, games against all of the

---

18 It is a reasonable assumption that the meeting with Findlay included Lord Harris, then MCC treasurer, and Sir Francis Lacey, then MCC secretary, and that the minutes for the meeting were taken and archived by Lacey. See 'Lacey's Lost Record' on page 89.

19 The English Test side until the 1976/77 tour of India was officially the MCC side. Speaking of, for example, 'England vs. Australia' in cricket prior to this time is an anachronism.

counties playing in the County Championship, as well as MCC, Oxford University and Cambridge University, a tour of Scotland, and several games against invitational sides such as HK Foster's XI, or CB Fry's XI.[20] The eventual schedule did indeed look a lot like a regular tour schedule, with the exception of not having any combined county matches, the customary tour of Wales, and no games against England. Lord Hawke stated it was to be left to the council who would meet on 13 January to arrange the fixtures.[21] It is interesting to note that the Test status of the matches was reported in South Africa, but the English and Australian press were still much more circumspect, although, as shown, it is likely that at this stage in January 1919, there was an agreement

---

20 In 1912, due to the tour being a triangular series with South Africa, there were only three Tests, but five was standard. The AIF XI did not make a trip to Wales as was customary.

21 It's unclear who Hawke meant by the 'council'. There are no official 'councils' at this time (the county cricket council having been disbanded in 1890). Everything at this time was a 'committee', and there was a meeting on 13 January 1919 of the MCC committee, which was the main committee governing cricket at the time, so it is likely this is the meeting Hawke meant. However, the fixtures are not mentioned in the minutes of that committee meeting.

between the ABC and MCC for the England XI v AIF XI matches to be considered Tests.

Lacey's Lost Records

Unfortunately, there is no record of the correspondence between Findlay and Lacey in either the MCC minutes book or in Lacey's personal correspondence that is still extant in the Lord's archives. There is no record that would suggest that Lacey's personal correspondence or archives were held elsewhere. What is intriguing about the lack of a record of this meeting is the obsessive nature of Lacey's record-keeping. It would seem that he kept *everything*. In the MCC archives there are dozens upon dozens of requests for tickets (members would write to Lacey to request a ticket for a certain game and then he would post them out) and people writing to ask for jobs. The letters between Lacey, Frank Iredale, Sydney Smith and others, organising the 1920/21 Ashes, as well as reflections after that tour are still in existence. Therefore, the lack of any documentation surrounding the AIF XI tour raises some questions. Unfortunately, no amount of research has been able to uncover a satisfactory answer to these questions. However, there is some circumstantial evidence that allows some speculation.

While there are some documents in Findlay's secretarial records from the period in question, mostly relating to the fixing of damage that occurred during the war, there is one notable file worth examining. MCC/CRI/5/4/1 is ostensibly the archive covering the finances of tours the MCC was part of, but in practice includes all of the documents that relate to tours between 1911 and 1948. In this file there are detailed records regarding the planning and debriefing of the 1912 Australian tour of England, the negotiations in 1914 and 1915 regarding the financial arrangements for future tours, and the negotiations for the 1920/21 tour of Australia. These are the international programmes that bookend the AIF XI tour. It seems reasonable that there would be similar letters regarding the planning and debriefing of the AIF XI tour, yet these are not to be found.

What is found in these documents that are nearby these is the strong smell of smoke, and evidence of smoke damage. According to the staff of the MCC archive at Lord's, there is no record of where archives were kept during the Second World War. There were several occasions during the Blitz where the ground was hit by German bombs, leading to several fires. Given the understandably chaotic nature of the time, and the equally understandable low priority of historical documents, it is not a large stretch of the imagination to speculate that the documents that would shed a great deal of light on the organisation of the AIF XI and the subsequent tour were lost in one of these raids. It is possible that they were just misplaced (the Lord's archive is made up of 30 cubic metres of documents), and may surface at a later date, but for now nearly all of the documentation of the tour from the English side has been lost.

Tour Finances

The full text of the telegram sent to the MCC reads as follows:

> Agree Test matches and full programme, 15 players, each £150, with manager £200 and expenses. Require indemnity MCC against loss, advise expenses, team much less owing to small amount of boat fares.

MCC interpreted this to mean the ABC would take half the gate, and if receipts did not cover the £150 for 15 players, plus £200, plus expenses for all 16, then

MCC would cover the difference. As noted earlier, the financing of international tours at this time was going through a major shake-up. One contributing factor to this was the overhaul of administration that had gone on in Australia. As the tours moved away from being privately or player led to administrator led the board was expected to take on a greater share of the risk. MCC, which had long underwritten tours to Australia, was beginning to question the value of touring there, as they had taken several losses in previous years.

The financial arrangements, particularly those surrounding the Test matches, could not be finalised until a meeting of the ABC had been called. At the committee meeting on 13 January 1919, it was noted that AIF HQ had promised to support the matches in England, although the extent of this support was not reported. Notably, there is no mention of this commitment in any of the extant histories of the tour. It goes a long way to undermining the argument that it was financial worries that brought about the dropping of Test status for the representative matches. It was also decided at this meeting to push the decision on sending an English XI to Australia in 1920 back to the meeting on 2 February.

Australian Sport Control Board

At the beginning of January 1919, the AIF created the Australian Sport Control Board (ASCB) under the control of General Murdock and Colonel Dodds. The purpose of the ASCB was to organise the playing of sport by servicemen awaiting demobilisation in England. This included 'Test matches between British, Belgian, French, and American troops in cricket, football, rowing, swimming, rifle shooting, boxing and tennis and general athletics'. Funding would come from gates but would also require public assistance to ensure it was spread out among all units.

Although Campbell and Barbour were widely announced as being on the ASCB in the media, this is not reflected in either of their war service records (as opposed to Massie and Middleton, who were also mentioned as being on the board). Nor are they mentioned in the official history of the board written just after the war.

The Troubles Begin

By the middle of January 1919, the AIF Australian XI had appointed selectors and managers to get on with the business of choosing a side and organising the matches.

Strangely, however, news of the tour went silent. Sydney Smith informed the media in early January that his expectation was that he would hear from Campbell in his position as manager and selector soon. By 10 January, Campbell had not yet arrived in London and Smith had not heard from him. Smith received a cable from Campbell in mid-January stating that he would not be available to act as selector and manager as he was returning home due to a knee injury that he was currently receiving treatment for in hospital. This is something Jack Davis had published in December, despite recommending Campbell in November; just another example of Davis apparently being more in the know than the administrators of the game. The *United Service* reported that there had yet to be found a replacement for Campbell. Although Campbell would be unable to tour, he would be available to assist with the organisation of the team while he convalesced in England.

It was also reported in late January that certain players were 'resistant' to Barbour, who was now a member of the Sports Control Board. The unnamed players urged the selection of a 'strong manager', even if he was not a cricketer, rather than Barbour, whom they regarded as lacking in 'business knowledge and tact'. They also rejected the notion of Barbour as captain, harking back to the pre-1912 notion that it should be the players who elect the captain. This discord was being reported as hampering the arrangements for the tour. Also causing difficulty was the fact that Roy Park had yet to arrive from France. This resulted in the situation that by late January, of the three selectors chosen to pick the side, one was bedridden in hospital, the second was in France, and the third was openly having his authority challenged by the players. When interviewed in early February by *United Services*, Barbour flagged that the tour may have to be abandoned because the 'players prefer going home'. However, in the same article it was noted that it was the lack of a manager, necessary to 'hold the indispensables together, smooth jealousies over, and negotiate with the Marylebone CC' that was endangering the tour. In other *United Services* cables at the same time an unnamed 'prominent Australian player' stated that the difficulties arising were 'insurmountable', that Massie, Macartney, Kelleway and Barbour were all entitled to early repatriation, and 'cricketers prefer to abandon the project rather than select a weak team'.[22] Although

---

22 Repatriation had started speeding up at this time.

unnamed, the timing of this information, coming within days of the published interview with Barbour, suggests it was Barbour who gave this background.

The ABC attempted to quell these rumours by announcing on 8 February that Major GS Down – not yet mentioned in connection to the team – would be Campbell's replacement as manager, although Campbell would remain selector. However, it seems Maj. Down had been approached earlier, as correspondence revealed following his appointment suggested the initial invite came some two months prior to the announcement. Sydney Smith also stated at this time that he was completely unaware of any reported problems with the tour. The ABC announced they were going ahead with the selection meeting in Sydney the following week, as always intended, but that this was being hampered by quarantines imposed by the outbreak of Spanish flu. However, following the meeting, the team had still not been selected – it was radio silence from Barbour and Campbell. But Barbour was not completely mute. Davis reported on a telegram Barbour sent to his father stating that he expected he would leave England in March, before the commencement of the tour.

This uncertainty was beginning to undermine the project. Frank Iredale, reporting on 11 February, said the end of the silence had been broken with the ABC announcements, adding that MCC were reluctant to announce the tour until a team had been selected, because without a thoroughly representative team there was a chance of a financial loss, as MCC had agreed to the ABC suggestion that the English guarantee the tour. It would therefore seem that the AIF's financial guarantee of the tour was not common knowledge amongst even the most in-the-know cricket journalists and insiders. However, confounding this was the almost simultaneous release of the proposed fixtures by MCC, with matches against all first-class counties, the Gentlemen of England, and three proposed Test matches.

Iredale suggested that if there were many players who did not wish to play it would mean 'disaster' to the tour. However, he doubts this conclusion, suggesting there must be some other reason. Iredale believes the player payments could be an issue. His understanding was that the arrangement was that all players would 'share and share alike; which is right and proper', but that some players may be 'hanging out for more' and that it would be 'a sorry day if any distinction were made between one player and another, whether on a question of caste or in regard to a monetary consideration'. Not only was there a question of payment, but military rank, which would become a noticeable sticking point later in the year. Iredale's belief in equality amongst the side was one that was widely held by Australian cricketing journalists, many of whom were former players. One report wrote 'if there is a real democracy it is in sport' and that 'a team cannot win unless all are equal'. The idea of class in a cricket team was 'repugnant' to Australians. Could it be that after four years of service, with rank enforced and being in England, a country in which social hierarchy permeated most aspects of life, that a handful of officers were willing to put their own social and financial positions ahead of Australian cricket? Could it be that in under 20 years Australian cricket could go from being player-led, player-managed and with equally shared profits, to administrator-led, with an appointed manager and differing pay scales?

Following the announcement of the schedule by the MCC, in late February the ABC received a cable from Barbour, Campbell and Findlay stating that Barbour, Charlie Macartney and Charles Kelleway would be unavailable for the tour. As Jack Gregory later put it, they were 'anxious to get home'. Additionally, as the MCC guarantee was conditional on a representative side, and without these three it would not be so, the tour must be abandoned. However, this ignores the AIF guarantee, further suggesting that it was still not common knowledge. Indeed, reflecting in 1941, when he was 'again captaining Digger cricket teams', Herbie Collins suggested that it was finance issues that almost caused the tour to be abandoned at this stage.

It is also intriguing that Kelleway was mentioned as being unavailable, as he goes on to be the initial captain of the side – perhaps offered as an inducement to get him to stay to make the tour work. Compounding these problems was another cable received by Smith from Maj. Down, stating he would have to decline the manager's position as he was to leave immediately for Egypt.

Writing in early March, *Point* could not find a clear reason behind the abandonment of the tour. He points to a 'vague cablegram' stating that there was trouble between the players because 'certain military men' wanted to retain their military ranks in the side. Sam Michael agreed, writing in reply to *Point*, '[w]ith the flannels on, cricketers should be comradely, even as they and their brothers were in the khaki days and deeds'. Jack Davis supported this view, also raising the problem that some of the best players were already home or on their way home, meaning a true representative side could not be raised. In England, the reporting vaguely mentioned the difficulty 'concerning the question of captaincy', suggesting it was not just the title and pay the officers wished to retain, but their positions of power over the enlisted men.

The AIF Take Over

Anticipating an ABC decision to abandon the tour, Col. Dodds immediately announced that the AIF would be going ahead with the tour without board involvement. Howard Lacy, MCC honorary treasurer and honorary secretary fixture bureau, was appointed as manager, with additional support from FE Lacey (MCC secretary) and W. Findlay.[23] Given the almost seamless transition from a board-approved tour to one organised by the AIF, it would seem that Findlay and

---

23 Note that both Howard and FE's surnames are spelt interchangeably in the archives, which can lead to some confusion.

Lacey, in conjunction with Dodds, were well prepared for the ABC tour to fall apart. One of the conditions of the military takeover was that it was to be an amateur side: i.e., no one would be paid for matches, although they would remain enlisted and therefore in receipt of their army pay (plus an entertainment allowance of 8s a day). All expenses were covered, and equipment was to be supplied, 'including three pairs of trousers, three shirts, one blazer, one sweater, one cap, and one pair of boots, also the requisite bats, pads, and other equipment'.

It was announced that there were to be several AIF teams, with the AIF XI being the best. As such there were to be no permanent members of the side; men could come and go into the team. Col. Dodds directed that the players would be available for charity and fundraising matches following the announced schedule, and that any profits made may be used by the host county according to their own financial position, although it would be appreciated if they were donated back to the ASCB who would be covering all of the costs. The implication here is that the counties could take as much of the gate as they felt necessary to shore up the financial position of the club, while leaving space for those few clubs in a solid financial position a way of avoiding any appearance of profiteering. And this did happen. Jack Gregory, reflecting in later years, noted that the counties 'acted generously and swelled the sports fund which was used to foster all sport in the AIF'.

With the announcement of AIF control, speculation at the cause of the collapse of the board-endorsed tour increased. The *Daily Herald* reported the 'difficulty' that had arisen in the formation of the tour was 'that officers and gentlemen will not be put on the same footing as privates in the team' and that they will 'not eat or sleep under the same roof as their private soldier cricketing comrades'. The reason given for this was the influence on Australian officers serving alongside British officers, many of whom had now 'become as snobbish as the British'.

Further supporting the idea that the reason for the unavailability of the officers was that as soon as the AIF took control of the tour, where one would assume rank and officer pay would remain, Barbour and Kelleway, along with Park and Pellew, who had up to this point been unavailable for service reasons, were announced as being available for the team, or the early matches at least. Macartney, however, was still to leave as scheduled, suggesting his was a genuine desire to return home to assist his family following the recent passing of his father.

Howard Lacy was now appointed AIF representative to the London Cricket Conference. In addition to his role as MCC liaison for the ABC, he had been trying to put together a team of the next-best AIF cricketers to tour the minor counties. With the ABC Test plan abandoned, Lacy offered to put his previous scheme in place, but using the best AIF cricketers and playing against better opposition. Furthermore, he also offered to guarantee the tour up to £2,000, an offer the ASCB declined as they were not able to accept it as 'they had special funds at their disposal to meet all requirements'. Lacy was given the authority to arrange all AIF games and Ernie Cameron was appointed to assist him.

Abandon All Rank

The normal run of play for military cricket was for players to retain their rank, with the highest-ranking officer being the captain. One such example was a game played at Tidworth in 1916. In the team were Macartney, Collins and Gregory – all past or future Test players. However, with the regular captain of the side Capt. Barbour away on leave, leadership was given to Lt. Fred Lewis – unknown to big cricket – as he was the next most senior officer. However, on the field, the cricketing tradition prevailed, and Lewis 'handed over the bowling operations to Macartney'.

Even though officer pay was retained, rank would mean little in the team. The official team motto was 'Abandon all rank, ye who enter here', taken from a sign above the doorway of Australian actress Dorothy Brunton's flat in Regent Street, popularly known as 'The Digger's Rest', an unofficial gathering place for Australian soldiers from privates to generals. Despite military norms Kelleway was elected as captain because of his prior knowledge of English pitches, not because of his rank. This abhorrence of rank within Australian cricket, called 'the freemasonry of cricket' by one reporter:

> … was sufficiently strong enough to overcome all the King's rules and regulations that seek to divide men into two classes – 'officers' and 'other ranks'. The field of battle knows its distinction of rank. The field of cricket in Australia knows none. The 'democracy' of the Australian army

> was much discussed during the war, but the 'democracy' of Australian cricket has for long been an accepted fact.

Even within the Australian Army some achievements were considered higher than rank. As one veteran Lt. Col. put it, 'you may take off your hat to any sub. who gets the Military Cross'.

All rank was abandoned within the team, except for on board the troopship SS *Ascanius* for the trip to South Africa, although during that journey the non-commissioned officers were promoted to warrant officers in order to get extra on-board privileges. The players wore their uniforms, with rank on their shoulders, throughout the tour. This was largely because they had no other clothes to wear. In the game against Surrey, Collins called all his team by their Christian names. This led some gentlemen observers to inquire with Jack Gregory as to whether Collins was a colonel or a brigadier: 'He was dumbfounded when I told him that Herb was a full blown "Digger".'

Writing nearly two decades after the tour, Bert Oldfield wrote about the 'Unqualified success' of the tour, in part because '[t]he spirit of comradeship that developed during those months was one of the most pleasant features because it brought together on one common level, officers and men of the ranks'.

Selection

The schedule of the new team was much the same as that intended by the ABC side, with the exception of dropping the Test matches. Fixtures were announced against all the first-class counties, MCC, Gentlemen of England, and Oxford and Cambridge Universities. Matches against Kent, Lancashire, HK Foster's XI and Gentlemen of Ireland followed not long after. Also announced was the squad for the selection trials. These were:

Gnr. EA Bull, LCpl. HL Collins, Lt. RC Coogan, Lt. CT Docker, Lt. JM Gregory, Gnr. RW Herring, Pte. D. Hotchin, Sgt. AW Lampard, Capt. EJ Long, Pte. GV Maidment, Gnr. JT Murray, Sgt. AW Oldfield, Lt. CE Pellew, WO. JF Sheppard, Maj. N. Spiers, WO. WS Stirling, Gnr. JM Taylor, Capt. WL Trennery, Capt. CB Willis, and Capt. C. Kelleway.

An invitation was published in the *Anzac Bulletin* and a circular was sent out to all units asking for cricketers who were interested in playing to submit their details. Many of the soldiers arrived in London in the last week of April and most were attached to the ASCB on 2 May 1919. The players were then transferred to AIF headquarters in London, and began selection trials on the Kennington Oval, which Surrey had placed at the disposal of the AIF XI.

Bert Oldfield recalled around 100 men showing up for the trial, but it was more likely around 50, with 16 finally being selected. His memory was that the final selectors were EJ Long, CE Pellew, and RL Park, with EJ Cameron on hand as an advisor. Jack Gregory remembered the selections being in the hands of Willis, Long and Nip Pellew. Herbie Collins put it as 22 men being asked to trial, with Kelleway, Willis, Pellew and himself tasked with putting the side together. Later, Collins said it was 100 men asked to trial, with Pellew, Willis, and himself tasked with cutting it down to 13.

There was one notable exception to those who put their names down: Jack Gregory. The Gregorys were famous in Australian cricket: '[h]e owned a name comparable in his own country with that of Grace in England'. His uncles, Dave and Ned, both played in the first Ashes Test in 1877, Dave as captain. His cousin Syd had been a member of the Australians before the war.

Several other family members were first-class cricketers, and his cousins Nellie and Louisa were the captains of the first two women's cricket sides in Australia. However, this cricketing pedigree weighed heavily upon him, and it seemed he would shun representative cricket, leaving a life in the city in Sydney before the war to work as a stockman in rural Queensland.

Jack Gregory was called to serve in late 1915, joining the 1st Brigade 16th Regiment, and made his way to England. Before he saw any action he was called on to play in several games organised by AIF HQ, including the Tidworth match mentioned on page 103. Although offered further opportunities to play in France, he preferred sight-seeing in the 'shell-shattered country'. His performances on the battlefield matched those on the cricket field where he was 'a tremendous force in the battery, his strength, agility and willingness in helping to lay the big gun being always quite a feature of that stunt. His earnestness and efficiency in his military duties soon led to his being selected for a commission.'

Jack could not avoid cricket – his billet for officers' school was the visiting dressing rooms at Lord's, the very same that had already been graced by Gregorys playing in the baggy green. Jack described it as 'like being home'. There it was that he was picked in a side to play a charity game for the Red Cross, later recalling 'everything I attempted that afternoon came off'. He was totally unaware that the opposing captain was none other than Plum Warner. Warner, on learning the 'long stork's' name was Gregory, asked if he was from *the* Gregorys, and said he had a future as a cricketer. But before long, he was called back to the 'great game' in France 'where both sides were definitely bowling at the man'.

As Gregory told the story, he did not put his name forward to be a part of the AIF XI. Rather, he was summoned; the word being that Warner had put his name forward, based largely on the fact that he was a Gregory, and therefore had to be good. At the trials Herbie Collins asked Plum who was 'the streak' bowling in the nets? Warner replied, 'I think he shows promise and has a good cricketing name.' It is for this reason that Gregory believes without his name he would never have gotten the chance to play for the AIF and would have played out his cricketing days on a dusty outback oval.

Initially selected as 12th man in support of Cyril Docker, by the end of the tour he would be an automatic inclusion on anyone's list of Australia's best XI, although Gregory himself intended on retiring from cricket upon repatriation and returning to the bush for stock work. However, at the insistence of Herbie Collins, along with most Australian cricket fans, he agreed to join the 1920/21 Ashes, and the 1921 tour to England. He announced his retirement in 1922, but was again talked out of it. He would eventually go on to play 24 Test matches, finally retiring in 1928 with 1,146 runs at 39.96 and 85 wickets at 31.15. His record of 15 catches in an Ashes series stands to this day.

Alec Bannerman said of his running between the wickets, '[i]magine that is a bayonet … and then say that the Aussies did not win the war'.

The final squad selected was: Kelleway, Docker, Long, Taylor, Collins, Gregory, Maidment, Oldfield, Trennery, Bull, Love, Herring, Hotchin, Lampard, Willis, Murray, Pellew, Stirling, and Sheppard. Herring, Hotchin, Maidment, Sheppard and Spiers, would not play in the AIF XI, whilst Sergeant HSB Love, Chaplain HFT Heath, and Staff Sergeant CS Winning would all play a role in the final side. Conspicuously absent from this list are Barbour, Campbell and Park, all of whom had been announced as available in the press in the preceding weeks, but were now definitely unavailable. Barbour had departed for Australia in late March,

Campbell a few weeks before him, having taken himself out of contention due to an injured knee, apparently unaware that he had ever been in consideration for any management or selection position. It is unclear why Roy Park did not play; he was attached to AIF HQ in London from February, but went on leave in April and did not return to duty until he departed for Australia in June.

Chapter 1

LG Robinson's XI

Old Buckenham Hall, Attleborough on 14–16 May 1919
Result: Match drawn

THE FIRST match for the AIF XI was against LG Robinson's XI, played at Robinson's residence Old Buckenham Hall near Attleborough in Norfolk. This match provides a glimpse into an era that had already ended, even if those involved were unaware of it: country house cricket. Having a cricket field at one's country estate had become a status symbol, particularly through cricket's first big boom in the Victorian era. Originally part of the gambling side of cricket, where wealthy aristocrats would field two teams so they and their friends could have a bat and a punt, by the end of the 19th-century country house cricket had become more about attracting the highest quality teams to your ground as a show of prestige and to host a prominent social event.

Lionel Robinson was born in Colombo, Ceylon, and educated at Scotch College, Melbourne. He initially tried his hand at a career in the public service, but found his temperament unsuited to government work and decided to give stockbroking a go. He was the right man in the right place at the right time. He had huge success during the mining boom of the 1880s and by the age of 22 had a seat on the Melbourne Stock Exchange. He found further business success in the Kalgoorlie mining boom of the 1890s, on the back of which he moved his base of operations to London, bought the estate at Old Buckenham Hall in 1906, and set about becoming a country gentleman.

One of Robinson's passions was his cricket field, said to be 'one of the finest in England', with a pitch made from imported Australian soil. And he set about scheduling games to match his social aspirations. His first major coup was getting the rights to host South Africa during one of their warm-up matches for the Triangular Tour in 1912. Old Buckenham Hall hosted several first-class fixtures in 1912–14 as Robinson set about making his case to host big contests, particularly hoping to get a match featuring the Australians when they made Ashes tours. The match against the AIF XI was part of his attempt to secure the opening spot on Australian tours, and he was determined to demonstrate the highest levels of hospitality. In doing so, Robinson was trying to bring semi-regular first-class cricket to a corner of England which had hitherto been unable to field teams in the County Championship. Norfolk, as well as the neighbouring counties of Cambridgeshire and Suffolk, were restricted to Minor County matches only.

The side for the AIF 'XI' – this was a 12-a-side match – was largely as it was to be for most of the tour, with the notable exception of Hampden Love. Despite this being his sole appearance for the AIF XI, his story holds some interesting features that tell us more about the AIF XI and cricket in the inter-war period.

Hammy Love was a wicketkeeper; however, he was not selected as such in this match in favour of the proven Ed Long, himself eventually replaced as wicketkeeper when Bert Oldfield made the position his own later in the tour. This would be a common refrain for Love, as Oldfield would also frustrate his efforts to play in the New South Wales side and Love spent the 1922/23–1926/27 seasons keeping for Victoria. His sole Test match appearance came in the fourth Test of the infamous 1932/33 'Bodyline' Ashes series, where he replaced Oldfield after the latter famously suffered a head fracture from the bowling of Harold Larwood in the previous Test. Love's reason for not continuing on the tour was he wished to return home for family reasons. However, he stayed behind in England to take advantage of one of the many training courses the AIF were providing for soldiers awaiting repatriation. Love took the opportunity to take a course in mechanics, quite the change from his pre-war career as a clerk. He eventually left England in November – after the rest of the team – although his direct route back to Australia saw him returning home first. His quest to be in the side was not helped by his batting performance at Old Buckenham Hall as he found himself beaten by a Pegler googly for a duck in the first innings and was trapped lbw by Woolley for 2 in the second.

But for the rest of the cricketing world this match was the first taste of what this Australian side could offer; a 'full dress rehearsal' on an 'alfresco stage'. A 12-a-side affair highlighted the friendly nature of the match, but, a look at the 12 men on the team list of LG

Robinson's 'XI' shows it was far from low quality. The bulk of the side was taken from Kent's county team: Jack Hubble, Jack Bryan, Lionel Troughton, Gerald Hough, Eric Fulcher, Jack Mason, Frank Woolley and Wally Hardinge were joined by Johnny Douglas and future England Test player Alec Kennedy, as well as two of the South African standouts of the Triangular Tournament, Sid Pegler and Herbie Taylor.

The hosts won the toss and decided to bat in front of the small crowd made up of Robinson and his esteemed guests, workers from the estate, and neighbours from the nearby village of Old Buckenham. The weather was glorious and the Australian soil under the wicket was fast. Taylor and Hardinge opened the batting but were soon gone. Hough top-scored with 30 as the hosts fell for 147 on the first afternoon. Cyril Docker, who had played one Sheffield Shield match for New South Wales in 1909, began answering the question of whether Australia's bowling stocks could be replenished with five wickets for just 34 runs. In response the Australians mustered 227, largely thanks to Herbie Collins' top score of 87 – Australia's haunted number – while Pegler was the chief destroyer on the bowling side, taking 5-54.

Robinson's XI dominated the second day's play. Hardinge held up an end all morning before being run out on 72, while Troughton and Hough sought to set the Australians a target with a stubborn 124-run partnership for the seventh wicket, Hough ending the day on 87 not out. The home team declared overnight, setting the AIF 282 to chase on the third and final day. Half-centuries from Willis and Taylor helped push the Australians to 274 for the loss of nine wickets – just eight runs shy of victory. However, in the big scheme of the tour, and low stakes of the game, it was decided at this point that the most sporting finish to the match would be a draw so the players could retire to the main house to enjoy the social features of a country house match.

The result was also great promotion for the tour. LG Robinson's XI was far from a bunch of boys, old men and second-class cricketers. This was a match worthy of international cricket. Although Kelleway had disappointed, names largely unknown to cricket like Docker and Taylor were lighting the beacons of hope for a new generation, and young pre-war talents Willis and Collins had shown their time at war had not dented their nascent abilities.

Robinson's scheme to bring big cricket to Old Buckenham Hall was ultimately successful; Old Buckenham Hall hosted the second match of the 1921 Australian tour of the British Isles. Unfortunately for Robinson he died of cancer in 1922 before the Australians could visit again and the property became a boarding school until 1956. The ground fell away during this time but was restored in the 1990s and now regularly hosts Old Buckenham in the Norfolk Cricket Alliance. A war memorial installed by LG Robinson in 1919 is still maintained by the Lionel Robinson War Memorial Trust.

Chapter 2

Essex

County Ground, Leyton on 17–19 May 1919
Result: Australian Imperial Forces won by an innings and 114 runs

AFTER THE relatively easy warm-up of country house cricket the team travelled to the County Ground in Leyton for their first match against a *bona fide* first-class side. After just three wins in the 1912 and 1913 seasons, Essex were a side on the up in 1914, scoring nine wins under the leadership of JWHT Douglas. Now, not only did they still have their great captain, but the side itself was relatively untouched by the war. Of the six Essex players who died in the war, only two – Harold Mead and Geoffrey Davies – were still active cricketers when the war broke out. Mead, son of English Test player Walter, had played four first-class games before the war without making any impact. On the other hand, Davies looked like a genuine up and comer. He was still a high school student when he made his county debut in 1912. For the seasons 1912–14 he mixed his county duties with first-class matches for Cambridge, notching up a massive 54 first-class games before his 22nd birthday. With a bowling average of 18.35 and a batting average of 20.81, he was on the way to becoming a genuine champion all-rounder for his nation.

This would be the match to set the tone for the tour. If the Australians could not compete against a middle-of-the-road, bruised, but not beaten county side, then the whole mission was a joke. If no one showed up to pay at the gate, then rather than being a financial boon to cricket, it would become an albatross around the necks of the counties. The latter concern was set aside when over 4,000 came through the turnstiles on day one. Big cricket was back.

Douglas was not the only star on the Essex side. Frank Gillingham had been a member of the Essex XI who beat Australia on the 1905 tour, and still had a decade of first-class cricket ahead of him. Serving as a rector in Bermondsey when war had broken out in 1914, Gillingham had left for the Western Front in late August, one of over 4,400 clergymen who answered the country's call by enlisting in the Army Chaplains' Department. In the Christian culture of early 20th-century Britain, chaplains would play a key role in sustaining morale by ministering to the spiritual and pastoral needs of their men. In an April 1916 lecture he spoke about another amusing duty of the army chaplain:

> Part of the duties as a chaplain was to censor letters. I could always tell by the thickness to whom they were addressed. Usually it was half a page to a mother, three to a wife, and seventeen pages to Tommy's best girl.
>
> A soldier was having his dinner at the back of a trench when a shell caused a lump of Belgian soil to drop into his billy-cup. Poking the earth out with a stick, the soldier remarked, 'I don't mind fighting for the bloomin' country, but I don't want to eat it.'

As well as humorous talks, Gillingham's patriotic Anglicanism led him to challenge those amongst England's menfolk not pulling their weight, or worse in his eyes, challenging the social and economic order by having the temerity to demand a decent standard of living. Having returned from the front in 1915, in a sermon in Birmingham in September he echoed the sentiments around 'eligibles' and 'slackers' heard in Australia, preaching:

> The patriotism of England does not compare with that of France. I have seen more single young men in mufti in an hour than I have seen in France during my whole stay. There are innumerable young men who ought to go to the front, but many prefer to stay safely at home to fatten and batten upon the good jobs vacated by men who had gone to do their duty. … It is deplorable that there should be any internal strife at such a time of national danger. To strike for 1d or 2d per hour was an enormity which should not be permitted. If a soldier shirked a charge he would be shot. That punishment should be meted out to all the shirkers and exploiters of public necessity at home.

Such publicly expressed wartime sentiments did not see any decline in the importance of the Christian faith in post-war British life, as church attendances showed a slight increase in the immediate post-war years. Gillingham articulated a religiosity imbued with a sense of national identity which had seen Christianity remain a resilient force in the lives of individuals and communities.

The Essex match was not the first occasion the Reverend Gillingham had faced AIF cricketers. He fought the good fight on behalf of a Clergy XI which took on an Australian XI at Lord's on 6 July 1918. Divine inspiration was in short supply that day as the holy men were bundled out for 67 and 50. The bowling of AIF XI members South Australian Bill Stirling (11-28) and Jack Gregory (7-54) was then enough to bring a nine-wicket victory in a low-scoring match.

JWHT Douglas was in many regards the poster boy of English pre-war cricket. Nicknamed 'Johnny Will Hit Today' or 'Johnny Won't Hit Today', depending on what side of the Ashes you stood, he won an Olympic gold medal for boxing at the 1908 London Games, before he had assumed the captaincy of the national cricket team in the immediate pre-war tours of Australia and South Africa. As such, his name had been associated with early wartime recruitment drives and fundraising efforts. In

December 1914 a list was circulated to the press of all county cricketers in the army and navy. It listed 13 Test match cricketers including Douglas. He also put his name to a list of signatories, which read like a roll-call of the Edwardian 'Golden Age', appealing for donations to the Prince of Wales's Fund: Johnny Douglas, Frank Foster, the Reverend Frank Gillingham, WG Grace, Lord Harris, Tom Hayward, George Hirst, Jack Hobbs, Gilbert Jessop, Wilfred Rhodes, Reggie Spooner, Plum Warner and Frank Woolley.

Douglas' name was kept in the cricketing public eye as he was named as one of *Wisden*'s Five Cricketers of the Year for 1915. His club, however, was not faring as well. The 1915 Essex CCC annual meeting needed a personal cheque written by club chairman CE Green, to the tune of £66 15s 8d, to keep the club afloat. The county arranged matches throughout the war against local public schools such as Westminster, Felsted, Forest and Chigwell. The Leyton Ground was given over to military use, with the Artists' Rifles OTC making frequent use of the facilities.

Douglas himself, promoted to lieutenant-colonel during the course of the war, would seize playing opportunities abroad as well as featuring in Warner's

Lord's and Oval matches of 1917 and 1918. In March 1916 at the Gezira Sporting Club in Cairo, a match took place between British and AIF troops. Some of the Australians were from the headquarters staff left in Egypt after the Gallipoli evacuation. This included Albert 'Tibby' Cotter, who unleashed a fast-bowling barrage to skittle the Douglas-led British opposition.

In the autumn of 1917, under the shadow of Mount Sinai, 'Australia' defeated 'England'. Australian troops were having a well-earned rest on the Mediterranean coast after months of intense fighting. Camped not far away were several squadrons of British Yeomanry. A British officer challenged the officer commanding the Australians to a 'Test match', confident of an English victory with a side led by Johnny Douglas. Having won the toss, the Australians were skittled for 57. The Englishmen's assurance of victory soon turned to despair as they were dismissed for a mere 4 runs with 'Tibby' Cotter taking all ten wickets. Sadly, this would prove the swansong for this most fearsome of fast bowlers.

1918 found Douglas serving on the Western Front. In a match 'somewhere in France' on Sunday, 18 August between sides that entered the field as Devon Dumplings and Somerset, Douglas scored 61 in a total of 283/6 as the Dumplings won by four wickets.

Towards the end of August Douglas skippered a Boulogne District side against a Calais District side on the ground of No. 7 Convalescent Depot, situated on top of a hill to the east of Boulogne. Boulogne had to fight hard to avert defeat, and in the words of future England captain Arthur Gilligan who played that day, 'that grand warrior, Johnny Douglas, was undefeated at the end of the match'. The grand warrior, having survived the attentions of the Turks and the Germans, would perish in tragic circumstances while trying to rescue his father from a shipping disaster in 1930.

Also in the Essex side was Percy Perrin. Perrin still holds the record of most county matches as an amateur for his 496 appearances for Essex. He was in the middle of his 538-game first-class career. Powerful but slow, he relied on his big hitting to make runs, which arguably kept him from becoming a Test player. His 343, made against Derbyshire at Chesterfield in 1904, remains the highest first-class innings scored in a losing cause. Perrin would later serve as an England selector, being part of the committee that made the inspired choice to invite

Wilfred Rhodes back into the Test match fold for the final match of the 1926 Ashes series.

Walter Turner was perhaps under-rated when walking on to the field. Despite playing for Essex for 27 years, being a career military man whose on-field appearances had to coincide with leave from military service limited him to just 51 appearances for the county. Another Essex journeyman in the side was John Freeman, who played in 337 first-class matches between 1905 and 1928.

An example of the weakness of the side was the call-up of Wyndham Hazelton. A regular feature in the Minor Counties Championship for Buckinghamshire, this was one of only eight first-class matches in a nearly 30-year career. Likewise, Bert Tremlin. Although an Essex regular before the war, he was 41 when he walked out on to the field for what would be his second to last first-class match. Also making his first-class debut was HP Waugh, who was still just 20 years old.

Most of the class in the Essex side was with the bat. It must have therefore been sorely disappointing for them to be bowled out for just 169 after winning the toss and choosing to bat. None more so than Douglas, who gave an easy catch to Gregory in the slips off Collins.

Turner top scored with 64 not out (dropped twice in his first over), followed by Gillingham on 29 (after being dropped on 8), and extras on 28. The first impression of the tourists was 'excellent', and Essex were 'pale ghosts of the old team'.

The Australians had surpassed the target before stumps on day one, thanks to a steady 64 not out by Kelleway and a quick-fire 78 from Collins. Kelleway would eventually be bowled by Douglas on 126, while Murray and Stirling joined Collins as half-centurions. The Essex openers walked back out to the crease at 5pm with a massive task ahead of them – score the 266 runs, and then some, to make Australia bat again, or grind through four sessions for the draw.

Promoted to opener, Freeman watched from the bowler's end as both Gillingham and Waugh saw their middle stumps sent flying by Collins before he was caught and bowled by Lampard. After Turner was run out, top-scoring Perrin had to stand by and watch as Gregory ripped through the tail, taking four wickets, all bowled, to leave just the number 10 and 11 to be cleaned up by Trenerry and Collins. All out for 151, the Australians were victors by an innings and 114 runs.

The gate of £110 was a healthy one, although all concerned probably hoped for a third day of play. For Australia, confidence was in order. Kelleway was still one of the greatest batsmen in the world, and the batting talent looked deep. Taylor, Stirling and Murray had all impressed. Collins, disappointing with the bat, made up for it with the ball, and in Gregory it looked like Australia had finally found their next Spofforth – a new demon bowler. The counties were on notice, this was a real Australian side. It looked like the concerns of the English may have been right, and that English cricket was not yet ready to stand up to the might of Australia.

Chapter 3

Cambridge University

Fenner's Ground, Cambridge on 21–23 May 1919
Result: Australian Imperial Forces won by an innings and 239 runs

THE LATTER half of May saw the AIF XI fulfil two fixtures that still found their way into the cricketing calendar right up until the visit of the 1964 Australians. Matches against Britain's two self-proclaimed elite universities allowed for a reflection on the huge loss of young men that the war had brought about. First up was a short journey from Leyton to the historic Fenner's Ground in Cambridge. *Wisden* recorded that the 'Cambridge authorities approached the resumption of first-class cricket with a good deal of apprehension, no one having at the beginning of the year even a remote idea as to the players who would be in residence'.

The hastily-assembled team included five men who had gained their 'blue' – by playing in the annual fixture against Oxford University – before the war. One of them – the Honourable Frederick Somerset Gough Calthorpe – 'Freddie' for short, served in the nascent Royal Air Force during the war. He would later be invited to captain England during their inaugural Test tour of the West Indies. John Morrison captained Cambridge during the 1919 season, on account of the letter inviting Calthorpe to fulfil that role being lost in the post. Morrison was a talented all-round sportsman, representing England at association football as an amateur and winning the Belgian Amateur Golf Championship in 1929. In 1914 he had hit the then record score for Cambridge – 223 not out against MCC. Like many, his university studies had been interrupted by the war, his time at Cambridge stretching from 1912 to 1919.

Arthur Gilligan was another player turning out for Cambridge University who would eventually assume the captaincy of England. He had been due to begin his studies at Pembroke College in the autumn of 1914, but the war rudely interrupted that plan. The majority of Gilligan's wartime cricket was played in the summer of 1916 when he was home on sick leave with an injured ankle. He returned to the front to see action at the Battles of Messines and Ypres in 1917. In August 1918, when serving as a physical training officer at No. 12 Convalescent Depot, Gilligan was able to get a few matches on matting pitches 'which were most enjoyable'. Towards the end of August, he was asked to play alongside Johnny Douglas for Boulogne District in their match against Calais. Gilligan recounted Douglas' words after losing the toss:

> He asked me to start the bowling, and I was very impressed with one of the opening Calais batsmen.
>
> He scored at a fine pace, and just before lunch was out for a very beautiful innings of 88. I asked the Calais captain … who this chap was, and he said 'Oh, that's Sergeant Bowley of the ASC' Little did I realise then that in two years' time we were to play together in the Sussex side, for Sgt Bowley was none other than Ted Bowley, Sussex No. 1 batsman for many years after the Great War.

Among the newcomers to the Cambridge ranks in 1919 was Gerard Rotherham, named as one of *Wisden*'s Five Cricketers of the Year in 1918 due to his performances for Rugby School. His team-mate, Geoffrey Brooke-Taylor of the Royal Field Artillery, had in the same year been awarded the Military Cross for his prompt and gallant actions. These men, and the other survivors of war, were left to reflect on those missing from the team that faced the AIF XI. The male population of the university fell by 90 per cent between 1914 and 1918. In all, some 14,000 men associated with Cambridge University served in the war; the Cambridge University War Memorial in Trinity College Chapel has the names of 619 former students killed in the war.

Among their number was Archer Windsor-Clive, who can claim the unwanted distinction of being the first first-class cricketer to fall in combat. 'Archie', the son of the Earl of Plymouth, had been tipped as a future captain of Glamorgan CCC as the county sought to attain first-class status. His seven first-class appearances for Cambridge University had returned modest success, his three wickets costing 72.33 apiece and his highest score in 14 innings being 22. A second lieutenant in the Territorial Army, he was transferred to the 3rd Battalion Coldstream Guards and promoted to lieutenant, leaving for France on 12 August. During the retreat from Mons his battalion fell back to Landrecies, where on the evening of 25 August he was killed by a German shell.

Another former Blue, Captain Geoffrey Davies of the 11th Battalion Essex Regiment, had scored two centuries for the county club in 1914, the second being in Essex's final match of the season on 1 September. Rather than return to his studies at Cambridge University, the promising all-rounder then packed away his cricket gear and volunteered his services. After experiencing the horrors of war at Neuve Chapelle in March, a comrade wrote of Davies: 'He remained as calm and affable as in civilian life.' He fell in action near Hulluch, France, on 26 September, aged just 22, one of 18 officers and 353 men killed that dreadful day. The battalion war diary recorded they were 'brought down by machine gun fire which sounded like the rattling of a mowing machine'. Initially reported wounded and missing, his death was confirmed in November. *Wisden* lamented 'there can be little doubt that, but for the war, he would have developed into an England player'. His body was never recovered and his name is recorded on the Loos Memorial.

Windsor-Clive and Davies were representative of the generation of men who would, in the normal course of events, become Britain's military, political and cultural leaders. One Cambridge contemporary of the post-war generation of university cricketers was JB Priestley. The Yorkshire man of letters had risen from the rank of lance-corporal to that of an officer in the Devonshire Regiment in the war, using his modest ex-officer's grant to fund a degree in Modern History and Political Science at Trinity College. In 1927, when the effects of the loss of a generation of fine young men were beginning to tell, he wrote of 'feeling until I die, the open wound, never to be healed, of my generation's fate, the best sorted out and then slaughtered, not by hard necessity, but mainly by huge murderous public folly'. Priestley's brother Jim had been 'blown to pieces at Passchendaele ... it was always fellows like him, the salt of the earth, who got done in.'

> People wonder what's the matter with the world these days. They forget that all the best fellows, the men who'd have been in their prime now, who'd have been giving us a lead on everything, are dead. If you could bring 'em all back ... hundreds and thousands of

> them, you'd soon see the difference they'd make in the place. But they're dead, and a lot of other people, very different sort of people, are alive and kicking.

It was against this dreadful backdrop of loss that Cambridge University took to the field against the AIF XI on 21 May 1919. Despite the admixture of pre-war first-class experience and future England talent, the undergraduates were demolished by the colonials. The first day saw the AIF XI rack up 518/7, with Charlie Kelleway scoring 168 in 190 minutes. His innings was chanceless, with his powerful hitting bringing him 27 fours. 'Nip' Pellew was more fortunate, being dropped on 43 on his way to 105 not out.

Clarence Everard 'Nip' Pellew was one of the babies of the side. He was still a student when the war broke out and had just begun to establish himself in the South Australian side in the 1913/14 season. However, as one of his generation's finest schoolboy athletes he had been considered a prospect long before he made the step up to first-class cricket. At the prestigious St Peter's College in Adelaide he played under the captaincy of Johnny Moyes, before taking on that role himself. He was also a star footballer for the school and played in the South Australian National Football League before the war. His nickname 'Nip' comes from his foot speed; he is widely credited as being able to run the 100 yards in 10.2 seconds.[24] Nip's all-round athleticism was on display when he competed at the British Empire and American Army Athletic Meeting at Stamford Bridge in September of 1918, coming first in the long jump and second in the hurdles. Often mentioned in the lead-up to the tour as an automatic selection, he would need to lean on this reputation as he was knocked out with the Spanish flu and unable to partake in the selection trials.

Nip's most notable talent was his fielding. Following the tour Plum Warner would consider him the finest outfielder he had ever seen as he put his pace to good use. Despite all these talents he only played ten Tests for Australia in two series against England and South

---

24 This seems to be an error in Pellew's *Wisden* obituary. Although he was a very fast sprinter, his 10.2 for 100 yards, time seems to be a misattribution of his brother, Lance's time, which he set both at the 1919 Inter-Allied Games in Paris and the 1922 Australian Inter-Varsity Games. Nonetheless, 'Nip' was given the name for his fleetness of foot. Lance also played first-class cricket for South Australia.

Africa across just 11 months of 1920/21, believing 'sport is important, but shouldn't take precedence over business'. He did have plenty of time for involvement in cricket off the field, however; he was the coach of South Australia from 1930–39 and again from 1958–70. He was the last remaining member of the AIF XI when he died in 1981.

Jack Gregory entertained the crowd late on the first day, smashing 17 off one Fairbairn over, including a hoist over the fence to bring up the 500. On the second day he confirmed his all-round ability, dismissing Morrison and Morris with successive balls, sending their stumps flying through the air. He bowled out five of the six wickets he claimed for 68 runs, before a strong last-wicket partnership between Rotherham and Naumann carried the students' score from 148/9 to 293 all out. Less resistance was forthcoming in the second innings, as the Cantabs were dismissed for 118 by three o'clock on the third afternoon.

Chapter 4

Middlesex

Lord's Cricket Ground, St John's Wood on 26–28 May 1919
Result: Match drawn

THE NEXT match for the AIF XI was their first visit to the home of cricket: Lord's. A Middlesex County Cricket Club combination of old legends, current heroes and a few also-rans meeting what was by now clearly a strong Australian side was the first big test of the competitiveness of the series. If the Australians could demolish batsmen of this calibre the way they had Essex and Cambridge then English cricket really was in crisis.

The number one batsman for Middlesex was Harry Lee. Lee would eventually play one Test for England in 1931, aged 41. However, he played over 400 matches for Middlesex and MCC over an illustrious career that included reaching 1,000 runs in a season 13 times. Lee was a model cricketer-soldier, enlisting following the call from his club and MCC. He was injured during the Battle of Aubers Ridge, and was left for dead in no man's land, leading to a memorial service being held for him. However, after three days he was found by German troops and sent to a POW hospital. Four months later he returned home, where he was honourably discharged and told that his leg injury – one now being shorter than the other – would preclude him from playing cricket again. He made his comeback in 1916 for an Army side and would have a further 16 years playing at county level following this match. Lee's opening partner was the aged WP Robertson, just a few months short of his 40th birthday, playing in his last season of high-level cricket.

The next four on the list are legends. 'Young Jack' Hearne was one of the greatest all-rounders of the day, although he took a season following the war to find his form again. Plum Warner's significance to cricket has already been lauded. Patsy Hendren still has the third-highest aggregate county runs after his contemporaries Jack Hobbs and Frank Woolley. Frank Mann only played five Test matches for England, but they were all as captain on the 1922/23 tour of South Africa, and he had a long career captaining Middlesex (his son, George, also captained both England and Middlesex, the first father-son duo to do so for England, and the only one to have done so for Middlesex).

All-rounder Nigel Haig was no slouch either. Twice a Test player, he did the 1,000 run/100 wicket double on three occasions during his Middlesex career. No relation to the general, he was, however, Lord Harris's nephew. The wicketkeeper Harry Murrell was getting towards the end of a long career, also being just a few months shy of 40. However, he was still considered one of the best wicketkeepers in the game at that time and was Plum's right-hand man in the management of the Middlesex side.

The final three were less celebrated. Mordaunt Doll was at the end of a patchy career, and Eric Martin was at the beginning of one that would be cut short when he died in a plane crash in 1924. The final player, Shearman Haslip, was an MCC member who made little contribution as a player, just being called in on a few occasions.

After a shaky start saw the Australians at 30/3, Collins (127) and Murray (91) hunkered down to add

187 for the next wicket. A cameo by Stirling of 57, including a stand of 66 for the tenth wicket with Long, put the Australians in a commanding position of all out for 370 when stumps were called on day one. The following morning Robertson and Hearne added 40s before falling in quick succession, bringing Warner and Hendren to the crease. They then put on a mighty partnership before Warner succumbed to cramp on 82 with the score at 275/3. The opportunity to run the old man out was on, but that would not be cricket. Instead, the Australians crowded around Plum and assisted him back to the pavilion. He returned after tea and dragged himself to a century, but then retired and did not come back to the field for the remainder of the day. This display of 'Empire Spirit' helped Middlesex to a first-innings lead of 38 runs, setting up an enticing second innings. However, only Kelleway and Collins – following up on his first-innings century – were able to get above 25 runs and left Middlesex with under 200 to chase. Time would be their enemy, as the match ended with Middlesex on their way to the victory needing just 51 runs with six wickets in hand. Not only had recent Australian dominance of the opposition ended, but they had been shown to be beatable.

That the war was over and sporting spirit was returned was shown by the barracking at Lord's. Although the practice disgusted Warner, even going so far as to suggest players should refuse to play in front of it, for many in the crowd it was a sign that the old ways were returning – one man complaining about the barracking ending his rant with 'it seems almost like old times to hear it'.

Chapter 5

Oxford University

The University Parks, Oxford on 29–30 May 1919
Result: Match drawn

WHEN FIRST-CLASS cricket returned to England after four fallow summers, it had fallen to Oxford University undergraduate Pat Rucker to send down the first delivery on 13 May. The former Charterhouse pupil was to play six further unremarkable first-class matches, including this against the AIF XI. His family would be blighted by tragedy. His elder brother Robin was killed in a flying accident at Amiens on 12 October 1918, while Rucker himself would be killed in action during the great retreat of May 1940.

With the match against the AIF XI at The Parks limited to two days, a conclusive result was unlikely.

So it proved. It was, however, notable for two debuts in the AIF XI ranks. First, Bert Oldfield was brought in to replace Ed Long, who had copped a blow to the face from a Jack Gregory delivery. The diminutive stumper found it ironic given the fact he had recovered from facial wounds received from shrapnel when he was fighting in France.

Oldfield, being completely unknown in his home land, was not included in any of the various lists proposed in the lead-up to the tour. However, he was invited to the selection trials, despite not having played in any notable matches during the war. It is quite possible his proximity to headquarters assisted in this, as he had likely played in one of the many casual matches HQ organised during the war. He was selected for the side, but Long was the first choice for wicketkeeper, with Love and Lampard ahead of Oldfield. While the AIF XI were playing in the match against Cambridge, AIF HQ were playing against Trinity and New Colleges at Oxford. Oldfield scored a strong century, prompting team manager Howard Lacy to send him a telegram to be on notice. A few days later, Ted Long took a rising Gregory bouncer to the face, putting him out of the Oxford match. Although already selected after the trials (albeit as a fourth-string wicketkeeper), Collins' recollection of Oldfield's entry to the side is a little more poetic:

> The day before the match we were searching frantically for a keeper. Anybody would have done.
>
> Somebody told me – I think it was the licensee of the local inn – that a young fellow named Oldfield was in the town.
>
> This man remembered that they had heard Oldfield say that he kept wickets for a Glebe (Sydney) junior side before the war.
>
> Has I heard of him?
>
> 'No,' I said, 'but where is he?'
>
> Nobody had heard of Oldfield.
>
> We combed the town and eventually found him. He was a slight, shy, nervous lad.
>
> 'How would you like to play with the AIF team against Oxford tomorrow?' I asked
>
> 'Me?' he said. 'I wouldn't be in the class of you chaps. Besides, I haven't got any togs.'
>
> "We nearly had to kidnap him to get him to the ground. Meanwhile we rustled up togs.

His diffidence was misplaced. Fearless in standing up to the stumps, even to Gregory's pace, his work behind the wickets proved as neat and meticulous as his fashion sense. When asked what was special about being called up to the AIF XI, he responded 'it's wonderful to sleep in clean beds and eat good food again'.

Although captain of Cleveland Street School XI – a position that had also been held by Kelleway – Bert did not consider himself much of an athlete as a child, preferring to wield the violin over the bat. But talent shines through, and in 1914 he was called up to play in the first XI for Glebe, one of the powerhouses of Sydney district cricket. He spent eight days in the brig in Egypt for 'neglect of duty [and] insolence to an NCO'. Although the latter would be a popular attitude when touring with the AIF XI, it probably explains why he ended the war with the rank of corporal. Oldfield caught a load of shrapnel to the face at the Third Battle of Ypres and returned to London to recuperate. Within a month he was diagnosed with 'neurasthenia', what would become known as 'shell shock' and we would now identify as post-traumatic stress disorder, leaving him unfit for front line duties. He spent the remainder of the war working for AIF HQ in London.

Despite these modest beginnings Oldfield became one of the revelations of the tour. Probably none of those attending the 1919 season saw in Oldfield's performances the early days of the greatest wicketkeeper of his generation. Although, a few of the wiser heads in the crowds noted his bravery standing up to fast bowling and the lightning stumpings that would become his trademark, taking almost as many scalps knocking off the bails as he did with catches (16 and 10 respectively in 13 first-class matches on the tour). His record 52 stumpings in a career still stands, six clear of Godfrey Evans in second place, and 14 clear of Syed Kirmani and MS Dhoni in third. His partnership with Clarrie Grimmett, off whom he stumped the batsman on 28 separate occasions, is almost twice that of the next greatest pair.

For the first three Australian Test series after the war – a home Ashes, away Ashes, and a tour of South Africa on the way home – he would share the wicketkeeping position for the Australians with regular pre-war Australian wicketkeeper Sammy Carter. However, once Carter retired, Oldfield did not relinquish the position for almost two decades, being the last AIF XI member in the Australian Test side when he retired in 1938, at the time arguably the greatest wicketkeeper in history.

The blistering heat of the first afternoon of the Middlesex match brought to Oldfield memories of wartime cricket in Egypt:

> You can visualise the great strain of playing cricket in the desert. The glare of the sun was terrific. Our pitch was made from wet sand rolled out hard, and the outfield, of course, was all sand.

The second debutant, the Reverend Henry Francis Trafford Heath, would have a miniscule impact on inter-war Australian cricket compared to Oldfield. However, his solitary appearance for the AIF XI allows us to reflect once again on the significance of religious provision in the Armed Services during the Great War.

Oxford University had a strong association with spiritual and recreational welfare provision for the British Army. The Reverend Richard Brook, a fellow of Merton College and future Bishop of St Edmundsbury, had taken a keen interest in the cricketing needs of his flock whilst serving with the Army Chaplains

Department. He issued repeated appeals in the press for cricket gear to be sent to the YMCA huts at the base camp in Rouen:

> The space in camp available for cricket is limited and so is the time. Some found that 'nets' was the most practicable method of securing the greatest happiness of the greatest number. Our chief need was for practice nets, gifts of which were few and far between. … Mud has a habit of hardening in summer, and campgrounds are almost always 'Unfit for play'; matting for the pitch was the only solution. So we would like to buy a lot of matting. Will any of your readers subscribe?

Spiritual sustenance was also high on the agenda of the Australian Army's Adjutant General, Lieutenant Colonel Harry Chauvel. An Australian Army Chaplains Department, similar in structure to that in the British Army, was formed in December 1913. The more diverse nature of religious belief in Australia was reflected in the fact that each denomination would appoint one chaplain general. It was proposed 116 chaplains be appointed, all at officer level. The four classes of army chaplain corresponded to the ranks of colonel, lieutenant colonel, major and captain.

Once war broke out, the denominational profile of Australian Army chaplains was based on information derived from the 1911 census. As was frequently the case when religion and warfare mixed, controversy was not far away. The Anglican Church believed their members had enlisted in greater numbers than men of other denominations – despite the actual numbers being almost identical to census records – and that this should be reflected in the spread of appointments to the department.

Far from the religious unity seen in England, the debate surrounding conscription – generally supported by the Anglican Church and opposed by Catholics – as well as split loyalties over the increasing tensions in Ireland, had brought sectarian conflict to a peak rarely seen in Australia. However, despite making up 21 per cent of the population, and 20 per cent of the AIF, the only Catholic regular in the AIF XI was Ted Long. This was largely due to the interaction between religion, class and cricket in Australia, which will be examined further in a later chapter.

Over the course of the war, 414 clergymen served in the AIF. Harry Heath was one of 54 Methodist chaplains to be appointed Temporary Chaplain to the Forces. Thirty-year-old Heath had joined the Australian Army Chaplains Department on 25 December, giving his occupation as 'Minister Gospel', and embarked from Adelaide on 16 January 1917. This was the earliest age at which chaplains could be employed for continuous service. No specific military training was provided, meaning many chaplains had little or no understanding of military life and culture.

With a very vague brief, Australian Army chaplains would use their initiative to do what they thought best for the men under their care. On the journey to the northern hemisphere the more serious-minded organised Bible study groups while others acted like superannuated entertainments officers, arranging sing-songs and boxing. Once at the front, more sombre duties included burying the dead, recording the details of the deceased and writing to their families. Church parades and religious services were conducted on a regular basis, with less formal entertainments including sports, concerts and lectures. Their remit extended to religious, cultural, ethical and pastoral care for the troops.

It is not known how Heath came to be invited to play in the Oxford University match, although it is probably related to the fact that as of June 1919 he was a student of the university, taking up one of the training opportunities being offered to AIF soldiers awaiting demobilisation. In September he married Scottish woman Irene Bain, returning to Australia in 1920. The couple come back to Scotland in 1926 when Heath took up a post in the United Free Church in Edinburgh. He was to play two first-class matches for South Australia, claiming 5-43 against New South Wales in December 1923 with his slow-medium left-armers. His victims were a roll call of Australian batting talent – Collins, Macartney, Andrews, Kippax and Kelleway. In his only other Sheffield Shield appearance he dismissed the mighty run machine Bill Ponsford for a duck. One can only speculate how far the cricketing padre might have gone had he devoted himself to the cricket pitch rather than the pulpit, but South Australia's loss was God's gain.

Heath played little part in the Oxford University match. In the undergraduates' first innings, it was Charlie Kelleway who skittled the students, his 7-47 seeing the hosts dismissed for 152. Kelleway declared the AIF XI innings closed on 391/8, with Taylor and Murray both taking centuries off the largely ineffective bowling. Despite there being time for 75 overs in which to force a victory, the Oxford batting, headed by Surrey opener Donald Knight, one of *Wisden*'s Five Cricketers of the Year from 1915, easily held out for the draw.

Chapter 6

Surrey

The Oval, Kennington on 31 May, 2–3 June 1919
Result: Match drawn

SURREY, THE reigning champions from 1914 despite not being able to complete their programme that fateful summer, included four players with Test experience and four *Wisden* Cricketers of the Year in the team that took the field at The Oval to take on the AIF XI.

General Birdwood was among the eminent military figures in the 10,000 crowd on the Saturday. In the match itself, the clever attack of Hitch and Co. reduced the Australians to 26/4, before Willis and Stirling pulled things together to get to a total of 230. Lampard should have been dismissed on 30, Hayes in the slips dropping two catches off Rushby. The Surrey captain rolled over and strained his right shoulder when falling trying to take the second catch.

In reply, Jack Hobbs returned to his pre-war brilliance to carry his bat for 205 in the Surrey total of 344. The great Surrey man gathered his runs with ease and fluency.

It was a relief for England's premier batsman to return to the pre-war rhythms of county cricket. His wartime years have cast a shadow over his otherwise illustrious reputation. 1914 had been his benefit year and he had twice achieved his highest first-class score. His benefit match, against Kent in August, was switched to Lord's as The Oval had already been occupied by the military authorities.

Hobbs was not one of the players who rushed to join the colours. However, his signature was among those of prominent players who appealed through the press for donations to the Prince of Wales's Fund in September.

The following summer saw Hobbs agree terms with Idle CC of the Bradford League – £5 per match plus £2 expenses. This put him in a different category to his county colleagues WC 'Razor' Smith and Herbert Strudwick, who had publicly renounced cricket for the duration of the war. Photographs were published in the press of the pair making munitions in a factory which had formerly turned out cricket bats. The *Leeds Mercury* reported: 'So keen are they in "delivering the goods" that they have forsaken sport and are now working seven days per week.'

In contrast to Smith and Strudwick, Jack Hobbs was eager to point out that taking a shame-faced approach to practising or playing cricket was 'ridiculous and unnecessary'. The England opener knew, in 1915, of one man who 'last Saturday carried his flannels to the local cricket ground in a handbag, and had his bat and pads done up in a brown paper parcel'. Yet the man was well over service age. Hobbs pointed out that just because a man was a professional cricketer, it did not follow that he would pass the army's medical test: 'The man who has been playing day after day for some years contracts strained heart, varicose veins, "athlete's knee" and kindred ills.' He admitted to owing his 'daily bread to cricket. … Would that I could now owe it to soldiering.'

He relayed an alleged encounter that had taken place a few days previously:

> I met a one-time patron of cricket who was
> driving a fine motor car. He stopped.

> 'Well, Hobbs,' said he, 'where are you off to?'
>
> 'Oval,' I replied; 'going to get some practice.'
>
> 'Cricket?' he asked, with uplifted eyebrows. 'Great Heaven! I'm surprised. Surely you cannot play cricket in war-time! Well, good-bye. I'm just taking a run down to Brighton. Road's in splendid condition. By the way, give me a look up tomorrow. Make it the afternoon, as I'm having a round of golf in the morning.'

Hobbs took his cue from David Lloyd George, who took over as prime minister of a coalition government in 1916. Lloyd George claimed the man who worked in a factory or in commerce was 'doing his bit', thus it was not considered 'bad form' to attend the theatre or enjoy other forms of relaxation, going so far as to write the preface for a book on the topic that was distributed to troops on the front line called *Doing Their Bit*. Hobbs averred: 'In the face of this, I cannot see what case there is against the man who prefers to spend a few hours in the pure air of heaven, exercising his limbs, to the many other ways of killing time in air which is not so pure.'

Hobbs bemoaned the 'half-hearted start' of the 1915 season, 'The grounds of most of our local clubs are deserted.' He had heard of one match taking place where the home side consisted of four men aged over 40, four young fellows rejected by the army authorities, and three soldiers home on leave. One man who had seen service in the trenches was tackled by a lady recruiter, who asked why he was 'slacking at cricket' instead of serving his country. Hobbs concluded that any man not of service age, or incapacitated from serving in the army, 'need not feel ashamed of playing cricket. Rather let him take pride in the fact that he is getting his pleasure in a rational manner and is doing something which will keep him fit for that day when his country may after all need his services.'

Hobbs's reluctance to throw himself energetically into the war effort might be explained by the fact that at 32 years of age and married with four children and a widowed mother, his duties lay on the domestic front. In later years, Hobbs would hint at having misread the seriousness of the state of affairs that he, as the leading figure of England's national summer game, might have been expected to show a lead in addressing. In his 1935 autobiography he ruminated: 'Like many others, I did not at once realise how grave the situation was; it was many months before I came to realise it.' Lord Hawke's resentment at Hobbs's role in enhancing the Bradford League's profile during the war would not recede. In 1933 the Surrey man complained that 'almost every year he has a go', as the aristocrat harboured a lingering grudge against the professional upstart who had refused to fall into line in 1915.

It was unclear what the nature of Hobbs's domestic war work entailed. Some sources have him as a foreman overseeing workers turning out cartridge bandoliers and other leather goods. However, other evidence suggests he may have had an administrative role, which would elide with the fact his duties left plenty of spare time for coaching at Westminster School and making repeated rail journeys to and from Yorkshire to play in the Bradford League.

His tenure with Idle CC meant that, in 1916, 'By road and rail, by tramcar and afoot, the people round Bradford were flocking to the Idle cricket ground on Saturday afternoon [20 May] for the purpose of watching the match with Saltaire,' as reported by the

Sporting Chronicle. England's premier players – Hobbs and Barnes – could be seen by war-weary workers for 4d, including entertainment tax. In the return fixture, Hobbs hit 87 before confirming his underrated bowling ability by dismissing nine Saltaire batsmen for 29 runs. Lord Hawke's mood would not have been brightened to read that this performance had earned the Surrey man a collection of £10 15s.

His team won the Bradford League title. Affectionate bonds had developed between the Surrey professional and his northern sponsors. At the award ceremony Hobbs declared, 'I could not pay a greater compliment than to say you are first-class sportsmen, all of you.' League president JJ Booth responded with praise, stating they had never 'had in the Bradford League a player who had become more popular not only on account of his cricket, but because of his gentlemanliness'.

Hobbs came across cricketers from the AIF in late 1916 in a charity match at Mitcham CC. He top-scored and took 8-23, including a hat-trick. Lieutenant AG 'Johnny' Moyes captained the visitors and the *Sportsman* reported, 'all these games at Mitcham have been characterised by the camaraderie shown by all concerned.' Money was raised for St Dunstan's Home for Blind Soldiers via entrance money and a raffle for an autographed bat. Mr EJ Callaghan, landlord of The Cricketers pub, donated a gold watch, which was wound down the previous day and 6d charged for guessing the hour, minute and second when the hands finally stopped.

The sheer destruction of the first few years of the war saw conscription introduced in Great Britain in 1916 to meet ever growing manpower needs. Along with these came military service tribunals, through which applications for exemption from service could be made on medical, personal or business hardship reasons, along with conscientious objectors, whose cases were usually not looked upon favourably. Hobbs appeared before the Wandsworth Tribunal in 1916. He was granted three months' extension from conscription 'on business and domestic grounds'. Hobbs cited his need to care for a wife, four children and a widowed mother, and that three of his brothers had already been wounded in action. However, on 11 October, he reported for military service and was allocated to the Royal Flying Corps as an air mechanic. His home service with the RFC allowed him to play a handful of matches for Idle. He collected a further £14 10s – a record for the league – for his century against Saltaire.

Such was the attraction of Hobbs to the Bradford public that the 1917 cup semi-final attracted a crowd of 10,000, with gate receipts of £110. This attendance matched that of the first day of the Surrey v AIF XI match in 1919. Hobbs also played in high profile charity matches in the summer of 1917, including appearing for a Plum Warner XI against a Bradford League XI.

The following summer gave Hobbs the opportunity to play some service cricket. Bert Oldfield, on leave in London, chanced upon an RAF camp near Uxbridge where a cricket match was in progress. Oldfield recalled:

> As we watched the game there was one player who stood out on account of his undoubted batting ability. Not only did he appeal to us because of his cricketing skill, but his immaculate appearance in his flannels – the hallmark of many an international – gave him a striking distinction. Never at any stage did he look like losing his wicket as he seemed to do just what he liked with the bowling and certainly thrilled the meagre

> collection of khaki-clad onlookers. We learnt to our surprise and delight that it was none other than the renowned Jack Hobbs. Imagine our excitement seeing such an international cricketer in action during the war days in one of the most secluded and prettiest settings to be imagined.

A little over two years later, Oldfield would find himself behind the stumps at the Sydney Cricket Ground as 'the renowned' Hobbs strode out to open the batting for England in the first post-war Ashes Test.

The resumption of the first-class game saw Hobbs return to pre-war form. He was the leading run-scorer during the season, amassing 2,594 runs at an average of 60.32 during 30 matches for Surrey and the Players. He was the only batsman to exceed 2,000 runs in the year. However, he recalled the 1919 season with dismay: 'It was hard work, and both players and public soon got fed up with the new arrangement. After a 7.30 finish, by the time one had dressed and dined, it was too late to go anywhere.' Still, Hobbs confirmed his enduring class by becoming the second player, after WG Grace, to score a century at both The

Oval and Lord's Players v Gentlemen fixtures in the same summer.

Hobbs's masterly 205 not out gave Surrey a substantial first-innings lead over the AIF XI. The second afternoon of the match, Monday, proved decisive as the Australian batsmen finally came to terms with the Surrey bowling attack and at 178 ahead with six wickets down it was left to a partnership of 110 between Pellew and Lampard to ensure the draw. 'Nip' had to retire from the field when he hit the ball full into his face. There was some disquiet in the crowd that Kelleway refused to declare with his side 348 ahead with three hours left to play. This decision allowed Lampard to complete his century, but was at odds with the dashing spirit expected of the tourists.

If the weight of his wartime reputation seemed to have been lifted from the shoulders of Jack Hobbs, Charlie Kelleway's standing took a pounding during this match from which it was never to recover.

Chapter 7

The Kelleway Controversy

THE MATCH against Surrey was Charles Kelleway's last on the tour. The reason why remains the biggest mystery of the AIF XI. Officially, Kelleway missed the match against MCC with a strain, and when his return to Australia was announced at the end of the month the reason given was related to the knee injury he received during the war.

Charles Kelleway made his first-class debut for New South Wales in 1907 but did not become a regular until his breakout season of 1910/11, which also saw his first selection for Australia against the touring South Africans. A decent average of 42 in that series saw him selected again for the following summer, although he was not as impressive in his second series in the baggy green. He found the English pitches to his liking when he travelled to the Triangular Tournament in 1912, coming away with an average of 60. This was second only to team-mate Warren Bardlsey amongst all three Test-playing nations participating in the tournament, well above the English top average of 49 for Hobbs and South Africa's Claude Carter who averaged 21. Given this was the last international cricket saw of Australia before the war, it is unsurprising Kelleway was the name on everyone's lips as excitement grew for the AIF XI.

Kelleway joined the AIF during the flurry of recruitment in the middle of 1915, enlisting as a second lieutenant in October after several months of officer training. He initially joined up with the 2nd Battalion in Suez, before being transferred to the 1st Battalion where he made his way to France. In July of 1916 he was shot in the right buttock and forearm, which although amusing, was serious enough for him to be placed on the dangerously ill list. After recovering, he spent 1916 training in England qualifying as a bombing instructor.

His second journey into the field came in May 1917, when he again went to France. He was in hospital from late January to April 1918 with gastroenteritis, and again from May to July with influenza – likely the Spanish flu that was starting to break out in army camps at the time. He was wounded a second time on 21 September 1918. By war's end he was fit, healthy, one of just a handful of Australian Test cricketers in England, and had achieved the rank of captain, making him the obvious choice to be the captain of the AIF XI. His early failures at the crease were made up for with several big scores across the following matches, but his decision to let Pellew continue to bat against Cambridge rather than declaring and trying for a result had earned him some criticism.

There are multiple explanations for Kelleway's departure. The *Star Green 'Un*, one of the newspapers that most closely followed the tour, went with the explanation that Kelleway had only originally intended to stay until June when he was due to return home. This is highly unlikely. Kelleway had originally been 'marched out' for return to Australia as early as February as part of the tenth quota to return. This means he could have left before the tour even started, but instead he chose to remain to play. It seems doubtful that once the decision was made to join the team, extending his stay by four months if June was the original return date, he would then decide to leave the team for the sake of returning three months earlier.

The most commonly published argument, and most commonly accepted by the credulous, is that it was his injuries keeping him at home. Kelleway himself argued it was due to a head injury he suffered right at the end of the war. However, the line out of the team camp, and that most frequently printed, was that it was related to his injured knee. No such injury is recorded in Kelleway's military records, although it is possible it was a more polite way to refer to his gunshot wound to the bum.

The most comprehensive tale of the tour written by one of the members was a series of newspaper articles published in *The Sun* in Sydney in 1941, written by Herbie Collins. The teaser for the series sensationally stated 'he writes also, of many hitherto untold secrets of big cricket – of incidents which would have shaken the sporting world had they been revealed at the time'. Collins introduces his version of the 'Kelleway Sensation' with the line, 'Now for one of cricket's behind-the-scenes sensations'. It is worth including his account in full:

> It was the sixth match of the tour – against Surrey at Kennington Oval. Kelleway was still captain, and, during an inspection of the wicket, he made a remark which offended

> a groundsman. This groundsman reported the matter to the Surrey committee. The committee took a serious view of the incident, and went so far as to communicate its views to the AIF authorities. Later a meeting was held in the Australians' dressing room, and I was elected captain in Kelleway's place. This was with General Birdwood's approval.

This account is supported by the one conveyed by Jack Fingleton in his 1958 work *Masters of Cricket.* Fingleton was one of the most respected cricket journalists of the 20th century, and would have had many opportunities to talk about this tour with those who were on it. Fingleton's account is as follows:

> It was during the third game of the tour, against Surrey at Kennington Oval, that Field-Marshal Birdwood, GOC Australian troops sent for Collins.
>
> 'Collins,' said Birdwood, 'I want you to take over the captaincy of this side from Captain Kelleway.'
>
> Collins was staggered.

'Captain Kelleway is a good cricketer,' said Birdwood, 'but unfortunately he quarrels. I understand that he has already had three[25] arguments – including one with the caretaker here before the game began. I'm sending him back on the next ship.'

But Kelleway didn't agree with the Field-Marshal. He refused to be 'sacked' and went to Brighton[26] for the next match of the tour. Collins approached him as he began to unpack his bag.

'Charlie,' he said, 'this puts me in a pretty awkward position. Won't you think it over?'

'I'm playing,' said the dogged Kelleway.

But the other members of the AIF team, after going into consultation, told Kelleway

---

25 Although it is unclear what the three are, it is likely that along with the incident at Surrey, the other two were Kelleway's insistence on retaining rank, and his decision to not take the extra 30 minutes on offer during the game against Middlesex, robbing the crowd of the chance of seeing a result.

26 The next match was at Lord's, not Brighton. Whether this undermines Fingleton's account to the point of incredulity is left up to the reader.

> that they wouldn't take the field if he did. So Kelleway gave up – and went back to Australia on the next ship.

There is no doubt that Kelleway was the right choice as captain initially. Not only was he the only Test capped player, but as he held the highest military rank in the team, it was natural for Kelleway to assume the leadership role so the chain of command could remain intact. However, as outlined in the introduction, even though the players themselves elected Kelleway to this position (endorsed without issue by team management), Kelleway's domineering attitude caused problems right from the start. Although never explicitly mentioned, most of the tensions surrounding rank that were prominent across the early months of 1919 seem to have been caused by Kelleway and Eric Barbour. With Barbour gone, Kelleway was left alone to fight for rank in the team.

Kelleway would play a further 11 Test matches for Australia, although he was never again considered for the captaincy, and he would never again play in England. He had his own 'Big Six' moment in 1926, when a falling-out with the board resulted in him not being selected for the tour of England that year. According to a 'non-playing delegate at HQ' the sense was Kelleway had 'the wrong temperament for a long tour'. He chose to go anyway – as a journalist – and spent much of the tour criticising the Australian selectors who had snubbed him and blamed the Ashes series loss on Collins, the man who had replaced him in 1919. Kelleway would only play one more Test for Australia, in 1928.

Chapter 8

MCC

Lord's Cricket Ground, St John's Wood on 5–6 June 1919
Result: Australian Imperial Forces won by ten wickets

THE WEDNESDAY prior to the match against MCC had brought the first rain London had seen for five weeks. Charles Winning, who served with the Dental Corps during the war, made his AIF XI debut. He had a dream start, having Young Jack Hearne caught with his first ball in first-class cricket. Hearne had, like Jack Hobbs, found the Bradford League a particularly welcoming and financially rewarding haven during the war. He had replaced Frank Woolley as the Keighley CC professional from 1916 onwards, having obtained 'national work' with a local engineering firm.

MCC's first innings was a melancholy one. Lionel Tennyson and Jack King were both out with the score on 7. Only Phil Mead, with 36, offered any real resistance in a total of 133. Gregory made 56 and Trenery 55 in the AIF total of 297, their partnership realising 80 runs in an hour. Johnny Taylor, described in *The Sportsman* as 'one of the bat-without-gloves brigade so fashionable with the AIF', pulled Jessopp into the Mound Stand for six during his breezy 31.

MCC mustered 228 in their second innings, thanks mainly to Mead (71) and Bill Jephson (63), who put on 110 for the fifth wicket. Bert Oldfield and Carl Willis knocked off the 66 needed for victory without loss, play going on until seven o'clock on the Friday to avoid carrying the match into the third day.

On the Thursday evening the AIF XI took advantage of their celebrity status to attend a social night at comedian George Robey's Chevrons Club. Robey had established the club to provide non-commissioned officers on leave a place to stay in London. Located near Victoria Station, it provided guests with a hot meal, bath, bed and recreational facilities such as billiards for a shilling per night. Robey, who had forged his reputation in the music halls, earning the title 'Prime Minister of Mirth', had previous cricketing connections. In 1917, during the match between Plum Warner's XI and an AIF XI, he had compered an auction of cricket memorabilia. These items had included a bat autographed by the English and Australian teams from the Sydney Test of December 1911 and the bat used by Wilfred Rhodes during his record 323 Ashes opening partnership with Jack Hobbs. The infamous 'bat of misfortune' was also up for grabs. This last item had been presented to Australian 'Demon' Fred Spofforth by Andrew Stoddart, with both men experiencing a series of low scores. Stoddart had met with the ultimate misfortune in 1915, the former Ashes winning captain taking his life by his own hand.

Chapter 9

Sussex

County Ground, Hove on 9–10 June 1919
Result: Match drawn

STILL UNDEFEATED and with Kelleway gone the AIF XI were becoming, in the words of Jack Davis, 'a band of flannelled brothers and most admirable cricketers with highly organised *esprit de corps*'. They next travelled to the County Ground in Hove to meet Sussex, who were far from recovered from the war. Most of the side was made up of old men who played before the war or those who only had the talent to be selected in these few chaotic years after. Captain Herbert Wilson was 39, with his best playing days behind him, likewise his opening partner, Joe Vine, a 1906 *Wisden* Cricketer of the Year. Bob Relf was 36, and George Cox was 46 – although he still had nine county seasons left in him!

The most notable player in the Sussex side was a young up-and-comer who had made his debut for the county in 1912 aged just 17: Maurice Tate. 1919 was his first of 11 consecutive county seasons where he would score over 1,000 runs.

Ironically for a player who would later be known for his strength and indefatigability, the 19-year-old Tate had been discharged from the 6th Reserve Cyclist Battalion of the Royal Sussex Regiment on 5 December 1914, a mere two weeks after enlistment. He had 'been found medically unfit for further service'. Tate was later to join the Royal Garrison Artillery as a gunner and serve on the Western Front, although few details remain about his time there.

In 1919, however, none would know that this hard-hitting spin bowler would hone his bowling skills to supplement batting slumps, effectively inventing the art of seam bowling. Tate did give a hint of it in this match. With the AIF chasing 179 for the win, Tate teamed up with Relf to take four wickets for just three runs to have the Aussies reeling at 73/8 when time was called: the first Australian loss would have to wait.

Although never seriously considered, in June MCC officially rejected the idea of sending a team to Australia following the end of the English season. Nonetheless, the Australian Board of Control sent an invitation in October. When declining, the English offered to send a team for the 1920/21 season if the Australians would return to England in 1921, which is ultimately what happened. For an English public starved of international cricket, the AIF XI would be the closest thing to international cricket they would see for years. But with Kelleway gone there wasn't even a bona fide Test player left among the Australians. Although those in the know knew they were watching *some* of the next generation of Australian Test players, they still didn't know exactly *who* they would be.

We have already spoken of Gregory, burdened with a great name and a sackload of talent. Plum Warner had spotted his ability the first time he saw him bowl in the nets, and now the rest of the English public were aware of his exploits. Those cricket nuts who followed the Australian season would have been aware of Herbie Collins, who already had a few seasons of Sheffield Shield under his belt, including an underwhelming match for New South Wales against the English on the

1911/12 tour. Collins had also toured the United States with Edgar Mayne's unofficial Australians in the middle of 1913 and with the official Australians on a non-Test series to New Zealand in 1913/14, although he was overlooked as a potential candidate for the Australian tour of South Africa that was postponed at the outbreak of the war.

Up to this point in the season, Collins had shown he was the business with the bat. His ten innings so far had yielded four fifties and a century and he had shown himself as a handy change bowler. In the match against Sussex he proved he could do more than keep it tight while the other bowlers had a rest, taking the opening pair of Wilson and Vine before cleaning up the tail to end the innings on 5-45, finishing the match with eight wickets. When the 1919 season was done and dusted he was sixth in the bowling averages, taking 106 wickets at 16.46, with batting statistics of 1,615 runs at 38.45. Taking the double of 100 wickets and 1,000 runs in an English first-class season announced Collins as an all-rounder of the future.

Chapter 10

Lancashire

Old Trafford, Manchester on 12–14 June 1919
Result: Australian Imperial Forces won by an innings and 157 runs

THERE IS an apocryphal saying attributed to the Duke of Wellington that the Battle of Waterloo was won on the playing fields of Eton. This is most likely a later attempt by the Victorian English to promote the values of 'Muscular Christianity' as something inherently English, as well as to reinforce the purpose and value of the aristocratic class system, particularly as applied in the public school to military officer corps pipeline. Unsurprisingly, the 'Gentleman's Game' was a central part of this cultural reproduction. Although the ultimate truths of these values were already being exposed by the Great War – ultimately to be swept under by the tidal wave of 20th century history – they were still very much evident in 1919.

As briefly mentioned in a previous chapter, one of the elements that complicated rank in the side was that it was top-heavy. Of the 18 men who played a match for the AIF XI, a full third were commissioned officers, another third were warrant officers or non-commissioned officers, with only a third still rank and file. The five captains in the team were previously in charge of up to 120 soldiers each. It could be said this was an officer side, not a side representative of the AIF. However, it is unlikely a preference for rank in selection that caused this, but the inherent class nature of cricket itself. This can be seen most comprehensively when we look at the occupations of the team. When men enlisted their occupations, they were entered as a W or B classification. These generally align with what was considered at the time 'white collar' and 'blue collar work'. These were much more the class signifier in Australia than aristocratic heritage was in England. Out of the 18 players, 16 (89 per cent) were W1 or W3 classification.[27] This compares

27 W classifications being white-collar, B classifications being blue-collar.

to the AIF in general, where only 22 per cent came from white collar industries, in itself over-representative of Australian society; only 14 per cent of men came under these classifications in the 1921 census. Only two were classified on their enlistment documents with a B occupation. One of those, B6 farmer Jack Murray was hardly from a struggling background, coming from a large landholding family in South Australia and having attended the prestigious (and expensive) St Peter's College in South Australia.

The term 'landed proprietor' was more apt than 'farmer'. The other B6 stockman was Jack Gregory, who, as previously mentioned, went to the bush in search of escape from his name as much as in search of work. Gregory attended the very prestigious (and very expensive) Sydney Church of England Grammar School. Of the 12 players whose school we know, eight of them attended elite grammar schools.

A strong but largely unknown Lancashire side met the Australians at Old Trafford in June. Former Test player Harry Dean was the most reputable player in the side, along with James Heap and James Tyldesley, who were at the end of long careers for Lancashire. The Tyldesley name was well known – John Tyldesley (no relation) had played for Lancashire and England, while two younger brothers, John's younger brother Ernest and James' younger brother Dick, also appeared in this match. Ernest Tyldesley would earn his first Test cap when the Australians made their first post-war tour of England in 1921, and Dick in the 1924 Ashes. Bolstering this were Charlie Hallows and Harry Makepeace, who would both earn their Test caps in the following 18 months, and Father Charles Marriott, who would play most of his first-class career at Kent before his sole Test match in 1933. Also facing the Aussies was New South Welshman William Farnsworth, who now added a sole first-class county game to go with his single Sheffield Shield appearance in 1908.

For Lancashire fans this match was an opportunity to see where the county's cricket stood. Unlike most English fans, the county's supporters had been able to watch play in the Lancashire League during the war, but this excluded the bulk of the county side. Opening the batting, Collins and Willis put on 117 for the first wicket before Willis fell, and after a brief visit to the crease from Taylor, Pellew joined Collins for a 99-run partnership. With Collins finally gone with the score at 259/5, the Lancashire crowd were probably hoping for a quick wrap-up of the innings; however, Trenerry played an anchor innings of 82 with the tail, leaving the Australians all out for 418 halfway through the second day's play. With so much time gone, the hope for Lancashire would be for a well-played draw, something that looked possible with Makepeace and Hallows at the wicket with 55 runs on the board. However, Hallows was bowled by Stirling who then went on a rampage. From 55/0 to all out for 125, the hard-charging Stirling took 5-38, well supported by Collins with 3-16.

With the more aggressive Collins now in charge of the side the AIF XI went after the win and enforced the follow-on. However, rather than going back to his first-innings destroyer, Collins tossed the ball to Albert Lampard, who aside from a six-wicket haul against Middlesex had been used sparingly as a change bowler up to this point. Lampard absolutely annihilated the top order, taking the first four wickets to have Lancashire at 45/4, still 248 runs shy of forcing the AIF to bat again. Gregory chipped in to take the fifth wicket, before leaving the rest for Lampard. In 25.1 overs he took nine wickets for 42 runs and embarrassed Lancashire totally, leaving them all out for 136, handing Australia the victory by an innings and 157 runs.

Albert 'Allie' Lampard already had several first-class seasons behind him when the war broke out, being a regular for Victoria from the 1908/09 season, and returning for several seasons after the war. However, despite being a fine all-rounder, he never found his way into the Test side, although he did tour New Zealand with what was effectively an Australian second XI in 1920/21. He has left behind little in the way of personal details and his war record is one of the smallest of all the members of the AIF XI, spending the majority of his time at AIF headquarters at Tidworth. Aside from a brief six months as acting sergeant, he started – and finished – the war as a private. His devastating bowling on this day remained his best first-class bowling figures.

Chapter 11

Yorkshire

Bramall Lane, Sheffield on 16–18 June 1919
Result: Australian Imperial Forces won by one wicket

AS THE longest day of the English summer approached, the Australians made their way by train to the Yorkshire steel city of Sheffield. The Bramall Lane ground had staged a solitary Test match in 1902, yet the contest between arguably the strongest English county and the best available Australian players had not always been keenly anticipated. The *Sheffield Independent* of 16 June reflected, 'When we heard that we were to have an Australian team we were inclined to look upon the visit as one of the least attractive of the fixtures.' However, an undefeated run had whetted Tyke appetites to be the first county side to lower the colonials' colours.

Seven thousand spectators crammed into the ground on a glorious summer's day. Batting first on a fast, true wicket, veteran Wilfred Rhodes and his younger partner Percy Holmes hit up 150 for the first wicket in 110 minutes. Both Rhodes and his even more senior comrade, George Hirst, were amongst the wickets and runs, the latter making 88 in Yorkshire's second innings.

At 3.20pm on the second day, victory for Yorkshire seemed assured. The AIF XI were set 170 to win. When their ninth wicket fell for 116 'it seemed any odds against them', recorded *Wisden*. Ted Long, 'a batsman of small reputation' according to one report, went to the crease. However, Jack Gregory was well set at the other end. For a full hour and 20 minutes the pair defied everything the Yorkshire attack could throw at them, 'playing with great nerve', eventually claiming the victory by one wicket.

The pair were given a sportsmanlike ovation from the Sheffield crowd upon returning to the pavilion. The Australians had shown they revelled in an awkward situation. Some local cricketers who had watched the contest unfold reported on experiencing 'exhilarating agony'.

One spectator had further cause for agony as the winning runs were hit. As Ted Long made his way to the middle he had shouted 'I'll bet you a fiver Australia is beaten'. The wicketkeeper clinched the bet and then strode out to bat, telling Gregory, 'A guy bet me a fiver we wouldn't do it so I'll hold up my end while you make the runs.' The bet was won and the pair saw that no one paid for a drink until a check of accounts showed £5 had been spent.

Ted Long had been a decent grade cricketer and rugby union player in Sydney up until the time he caught typhoid fever in 1910. Upon recovering, the then 27-year-old returned to wicketkeeping for North Sydney. In a match against Nowra he played a part in eight wickets in an innings, taking seven stumpings and a catch, at the time the world record in a grade cricket match. This put him on the selectors' radar and when 'The Prince of Wicketkeepers' Hanson 'Sammy' Carter was injured before the New South Wales v South Australia Sheffield Shield match in December 1911, Ted got his call-up. Although he 'kept wicket ably', his performance was nowhere near enough to dislodge the New South Wales captain, and the rest of his first-class career would take place on this tour.

Long spent most of his time in the war serving in the Anzac Provost Corps. The Provost Corps did undertake some espionage, but was mostly the military police service for Australian troops stationed in England. Although the Provost Corps saw some action, most of Long's service would have been directing traffic around Tidworth or keeping a lid on raucous troops out on the town.

Carter did not serve, and Oldfield was yet to be discovered, so Long was the natural choice for wicketkeeper in the first AIF XI side. Once the tour was over he was not even in the conversation between Oldfield and Carter, and given both of them were New South Welshmen he had to be content with just writing about big cricket, joining the 1921 Australians on their tour of England and South Africa, sending home reports under the title 'EJ Long, Wicket-keeper with the AIF team'.

Yorkshire, who would finish county champions in 1919, acquitted themselves admirably against the tourists. The club had survived a turbulent period of war. George Hirst, who according to one newspaper, had shown 'magnificent resource during a difficult time' during Yorkshire's second innings, was one of the professionals paid a retainer by the county club during the war years. Alongside Wilfred Rhodes, David

Denton and Alonzo Drake, the professional quartet were expected to undertake domestic war work. Clubs across Yorkshire could submit written requests for one of their professionals to make a one-off appearance in a local club fixture, thus allowing cricket followers across the county the chance of seeing one of the stars in action.

Despite having minimal impact on the AIF match with scores of 13 and 0, Herbert Sutcliffe was a young Yorkshire player on the rise. During the war, Sutcliffe had resorted to subterfuge in order to play high-level cricket. He contrived to play for Pudsey St Lawrence CC in the Bradford League under an assumed name. The future Yorkshire and England opener managed to reconcile his Congregationalist upbringing with taking unofficial leave. 'On Saturday afternoons I cycled the 20 miles from York to the Leeds tram terminus near Killingbeck, deposited my cycle there, and travelled on to Pudsey by tram.'

Whilst Yorkshire county cricketers served on the domestic front with distinction, the loss of Second-Lieutenant Major Booth (Major by name, not rank), killed in action on the first day of the Battle of the Somme, had robbed Yorkshire and England of a potentially great all-rounder. Bingley-born Arthur

Dolphin, the Yorkshire stumper who appeared against the AIF XI, had endured an eventful war serving in the Leeds Pals alongside team-mate Roy Kilner. Dolphin was wounded in action three times, the final occasion being in 1917 when he had received shrapnel wounds in the right wrist and left arm.

Yorkshire, like most other county clubs, had seen its share of tragic loss of a few and war service from most of its players. However, the large fly in the ointment of Yorkshire's wartime cricket had come in the form of the Bradford League, and its ebullient president JJ Booth (no relation to Major Booth).

The intricate network of competitive cricket leagues which covered Yorkshire before the war reacted in several different ways to the coming of war. Some cancelled all competitions, encouraging member clubs to engage in friendly-only matches. But the Bradford League seized on the lack of competitive cricket at county and club level to establish itself as a major focus of wartime cricket. This led Booth into a very bitter and public conflict with Yorkshire CCC and MCC president Lord Hawke.

His Lordship had decreed in 1914 that all competitive cricket should cease and the game's full focus should be on the war effort. Booth, on the other hand, was vociferous in his belief that the most valuable contribution Bradford cricket could make was to provide the best entertainment featuring the best players available in order to lift the spirits of war-weary factory workers.

Yorkshire's eight victories since the formal organisation of a championship in 1890 owed much to the layers of competitive leagues which adorned most towns and cities across the three ridings. The Bradford League – in operation since 1903 – was the strongest of the leagues in both playing and financial terms. 'To play or not to play' was the Shakespearian invocation of JJ Booth, at a special meeting held at the city's Market Tavern in September 1914 to discuss the following season's prospects. Whilst some clubs thought it better to cease operations for the duration, Booth remained steadfast in his determination to provide relaxation and recreation for war workers. Controversy would explode over the Yorkshire press the following spring as the consequences of Booth's resolve played out.

In fact, the Bradford League would go further by soaking up cricketing talent which would have otherwise been left idle by the abeyance of the County Championship and the policy of other leagues not to employ professionals. It was thus that Bradford would become the cricketing epicentre of wartime Britain. Leading lights of English cricket, including Jack Hobbs, Sydney Barnes, Frank Woolley and Jack Hearne made their way northwards to earn appearance fees and talent money.

Lord Hawke, an eighth-generation aristocrat, resented the cheek of the *arriviste* league in flouting his declaration. Booth reacted angrily in June 1915 to the contention printed in the *Yorkshire Post* – probably published at His Lordship's behest – that 'The playing of competitive spectacular cricket [is] not seemly in wartime' and the disobeying of Lord Hawke's 'Unequivocal dictum as the head of the cricket world [was] scandalous'. Booth noted, far from acting as a disincentive to recruitment, 'Recruiting in Bradford has been brisker and better since the cricket seasons commenced.' Furious telegrams and telephone calls were exchanged between Booth and Frederick Toone, secretary of Yorkshire CCC, who sought an emollient path out of the impasse, claiming, somewhat unconvincingly, that Hawke had been misquoted. Eventually, Booth succeeded in having the *Yorkshire Post* withdraw the 'scandalous' soubriquet from its judgement.

Booth disparaged the Yorkshire Council, which had decided to desist from league cricket, claiming,

'The Bradford Cricket League, and not the Yorkshire Council, have chosen the better part.' Stingingly he asserted, 'Our standard of "serious-minded patriotism" has been higher, and our foresight clearer.' If clicks at the turnstiles were the measure of who won the argument, Booth was victorious. A record league crowd of 6,400 paid their three shillings to watch Barnes' debut for Saltaire at Bowling Old Lane on 8 May 1915.

The keenness of greats like Hobbs and Barnes to find the most competitive cricket stage they could was not shared by many cricket followers. In a letter to the *Sheffield Evening Telegraph* Mr H. Sinclair of Rotherham heaped scorn upon the cricketers of the Mexborough and District League, pointing out only 2.5 per cent of the men in the district covered by the league had joined up, a figure unfavourably compared to between 8 and 10 per cent in some southern counties. He sarcastically wrote: 'There is, however, something the district ... can swank about, viz. there are ten flourishing cricket clubs in the district.' He scorned the members who meant to 'have a jolly time at Wath when the champion match is to be played'. Referring to the 2.5 per cent who would not be playing, Fisher wrote, 'And what have they been doing in the meantime? Reply: Fighting and bleeding for their

King and Country. And now, Messrs Mexborough and District Cricket League members … what have you been doing? Answer: We have been playing cricket.'

By mid-1916 a fragile peace was established between Yorkshire CCC and the Bradford League. The two organisations arranged a charity match for 14 August, which raised £170 for the Bradford Soldiers' Comforts Fund. JJ Booth, never one to downplay the excellence of the league, claimed his XI represented the strongest team put out by any local cricketing organisation. At the league's December annual meeting, Booth returned once again to the contentious claim that the continuation of high-class cricket would interfere with recruiting, citing there were over 1,000 members of various league clubs serving with the forces.

Still competitive cricket retained something of an unmentionable status in the minds of many of the game's followers, even in the Yorkshire heartland of cricket leagues. 'I should not like in years to come to show a cricket medal with 1917 on it,' opined one Yorkshire Cricket Council committee member in April. 'Who could be proud of winning such a medal in the present wartime? We are trying to keep the game alive, not win championship medals.'

However, by 1918, £2,597 had been raised for charities and war funds via Bradford League matches. Still nursing the emotional wounds from his bitter struggles with Lord Hawke and others from the start of the war, Booth jibed, 'Most of our short-sighted critics of three and four years ago are now dumb. Others, more courageous and sportsmanlike, are publicly approving our policy … our achievements have conquered criticism.'

The termination of the war saw the competitive leagues in the Midlands and the north resume regular competitions. However, the generous remuneration for a relatively light playing load on offer to the best players were deemed a threat to the status of county cricket. The most prominent league clubs regularly attracted spectators in their thousands and county secretaries feared the enticement of the best professional players away from county cricket. In December 1919 the MCC Advisory Committee decided that no player would be selected for representative matches such as Players v Gentlemen or an overseas tour unless he pledged to prioritise county cricket.

The matter did not rest there. In 1921 Lord Hawke, still nursing the bruises of his long-running wartime feud with JJ Booth and the Bradford League, accused Lancashire League clubs of poaching county professionals. In reply, the league's secretary claimed that spectators had the right to see the best cricketers. The following year Hawke complained league cricket was a 'real competitor' to county cricket. Despite these fears, very few big names decided to opt for league contracts. The most prominent was Sydney Barnes, who continued his association with Saltaire CC. The wartime ascendancy of the Bradford League proved temporary, with the county club which met the Australian Imperial Forces XI at Bramall Lane in June 1919 the undoubted king of the Yorkshire cricket scene.

Chapter 12

Hampshire

County Ground, Southampton on 20–21 June 1919
Result: Match drawn

HAMPSHIRE HAD their best ever season in 1914, winning 13 and drawing 11 of their 28 Championship matches. But the impact of war was soon felt in this most military of English counties. The United Services Ground at Portsmouth was rendered unavailable and the Portsmouth Cricket Week scheduled for late August was cancelled 'owing to unforeseen circumstances' on 12 August, although the games were moved to other grounds.

This came just days after the MCC meeting that had decided to push ahead with the County Championship following the outbreak of war. By 15

August the reason for the cancellation of the Cricket Week was 'obvious'.

Club officials quickly suggested a corps of cricketers should be formed to take their part in national service for the purposes of home defence. However, this suggestion was described by *Britain Uber Alles*, an anonymous correspondent to the *Sportsman* as 'A sort of move at best. "We don't mind doing something at the end of August after we've finished our game"' but this was a 'selfish song … Cricketers have done Cricket irreparable damage'. Further down Hampshire's cricketing chain, members of the St Mary's Cricket Club, Southampton, marched up to the headquarters of the 5th Battalion Hampshire Regiment en masse and enlisted for foreign service.

Criticism of the continuation of the game had hit hard. JC Moberley, Hampshire's president, and the club's secretary, Russell Bencraft, wrote to the *Bournemouth Guardian* on 5 September setting out justifications of positions taken so far. First, MCC was correct to continue the season for the benefit of professional cricketers who had signed contracts. Second, their own county had incurred heavy financial losses in doing so. Third, ten amateurs who had represented the county that season were already at the front or had been accepted for home service. The club's captain, Edward Sprot, had enrolled as a special constable. In conclusion:

> ... it is therefore perfectly clear that so far as the Hampshire County Club and its Executive are concerned there has been no lack of loyalty towards the pressing needs of the Empire, and we feel sure the same loyal spirit animates every other county club in this country.

A week later, two Hampshire professionals, F. Clark and A. Blacklidge, had followed the example set by their comrades and joined the 5th Hants Territorial Regiment. Seven of the eight Hampshire 'pros' who first presented themselves were accepted for service, but Phil Mead failed to pass the medical owing to varicose veins in one leg. Further woe would befall Mead in 1915, as burglars broke into his home and stole jewels worth £100. Many of the treasures had been brought home for his wife, souvenirs of his tours with England of South Africa and Australia.

Before 1914 was out, four cricketers who had appeared for Hampshire had perished in the war –

Evelyn Bradford, Arthur Byng, John Gregory and Geoffrey Toynbee. A further eight were lost in 1915, including Arthur Jaques. Jaques had been in fine form in 1914, taking 117 first-class wickets at 18.69. The 1915 *Wisden* described his bowling style:

> swinging in and getting … an off-break. Jaques pitches on the wicket or outside the leg stump and, with a bunch of fieldsmen crowded close in on the left side, he so cramped the batsman that sooner or later he exhausted his patience and so secured many victims.

Jaques had taken ten wickets in a match on three occasions during his short career. After receiving a commission in the West Yorkshire Regiment, Captain Jaques vanished from the world at the Battle of Loos on 27 September. His body – as with thousands of others who fell in that dreadful battle – would never be identified and he is commemorated on the Loos Memorial.

Hampshire's 1916 annual report celebrated a reduction in the club's deficit from £887 to £489. The annual general meeting was not recorded by the club's dutiful secretary, Francis Bacon. Serving at the rank of assistant paymaster on HMY *Aries*, Bacon lost his life at sea on 31 October 1915 when the vessel hit a mine off the Belgian coast. The body of Bacon, who had also played 75 matches for the county, drifted across the North Sea, eventually washing ashore on the Danish coast. He is one of two Commonwealth War burials in Borsmose churchyard in West Jutland.

Hampshire valour was on display on the battlefield too. Lionel Tennyson, serving with the Rifle Brigade, was thrice wounded and twice mentioned in dispatches. His younger brother Harold had been killed in January 1916. Alexander Johnston had played 107 matches for Hampshire between his duties as an officer with the Worcestershire Regiment. In 1914 he took part in the engagements at Mons, Le Cateau, and the retreat to the Aisne. Serving as a signals officer for 7 Infantry Brigade, he received the first of four wounds he would sustain during the war. Johnston, a useful batsman and occasional leg-break bowler, earned the DSO with bar, was mentioned in dispatches on five occasions, and had risen to the rank of brigadier general. Despite sustaining a permanent limp from various injuries, Johnston managed to continue his sporting activities post-war, playing one final match for Hampshire in 1919 and making further appearances for MCC and the Gentlemen. However, his regular first-class career was at an end.

Another player with a distinguished war record was Major AJ 'Jack' Evans RFC, who played seven times as an irregular for Hampshire between 1908 and 1920. Initially serving in the Intelligence Corps due to his fluency in German derived from a year spent in that country, he joined No. 3 Squadron RFC as an aerial observer. This pioneering role saw Evans take photographs of enemy positions from his flimsy aircraft at low altitudes, exposing him to enemy fire. Evans was awarded the MC in September 1915 for continuing to observe while under fire and was mentioned in dispatches. Evans was shot down on 16 July 1916 when undertaking a flight over German positions during the Battle of the Somme. Evans and his observer, Lieutenant Long, crash-landed behind enemy lines and it proved to be several months before they were reported as having been taken prisoner.

Evans would prove to be one of the most challenging prisoners taken by the Germans. He escaped from Clausthal before being recaptured close to the Dutch border and sent to Ingolstadt, alongside other officers with failed escape attempts behind them. In 1917 he finally succeeded in evading the Germans' grasp, walking 18 nights into neutral Switzerland with another officer. Evans would subsequently be transferred to Palestine where, once again, he fell into enemy hands, this time the Ottoman Turks. He bribed a doctor to place him on the sick list to be included in an officer exchange, being released shortly before the Armistice on the Western Front.

He was awarded a bar to his MC for his repeated escape attempts. He later wrote:

> I don't think there is anything I have ever done quite so exciting as escaping from a prison. … After all that, what thrill is there to be had in ceaseless seasons of cricket? And what fear to be found in facing down Ted McDonald's fast bowling?

Evans would become one of an unprecedented 30 players given a run out by England in the 1921 Ashes series. Selected on the basis that their wartime pluck would transfer successfully to seeing off the threat of a rather more friendly foe, several of those awarded England caps would make but a fleeting impact on the international scene. In Evans's sole Test appearance, scores of 4 and 14 would be his lot.

Harold Forster had taken 9-92 on his Hampshire debut in 1911. Forster was one of the most decorated first-class cricketers; a DSO and bar, an MC and bar, and five times mentioned in despatches.[28] Forster had joined the Royal Marines in 1897. A career soldier, he had landed in France with the British Expeditionary Force in August 1914. His various citations referred to a 'very gallant ... officer', 'pluck and energy', 'conspicuous gallantry and devotion to duty', 'a fine example of fearlessness and contempt for danger' and 'a fine example of courage and resource for all'. Although his death occurred on 29 May 1918, it was not until 23 March 1919 that his family had this tragic news confirmed. His remains were found during the extensive post-war efforts to locate and identify the bodies that lay with no known grave and today rests in the Terlincthun British Cemetery at Wimille on the outskirts of Boulogne.

---

28 John Smyth, with a Victoria Cross, was the more decorated soldier; however, his two matches for the Europeans at Lahore in 1923 are of dubious first-class status.

Although county cricket was out of the question in Hampshire, village clubs sought to continue some form of activity. Aside from the county club, Hampshire cricketers and administrators grappled with the hitherto unanswered question of should cricket continue in an era of total war? The 1915 annual meeting of Westbourne CC was presided over by the Reverend LB Birkett at the appropriately named Cricketers' Arms. In view of the war it was decided not to draw up any fixture list for the year, but friendlies would be played if they could be conveniently arranged.

The Deanery Cricket Club decided to arrange matches with military teams in the Southampton area. However, club president the Reverend Neville Lovett thought any players eligible for military service should be barred from playing unless they had joined up. 'Quite right, too!' exclaimed the *Hampshire Advertiser*. The young men who usually played on the parks and commons 'are needed for a higher and nobler game now'. Hampshire saw a large influx of troops during the early months of 1915. In order to cater for their recreational needs Hampshire CCC placed the pitches at the County Ground at the disposal of the military authorities.

The cricket correspondent of the *Hampshire Advertiser* opined 'in view of the present condition of affairs, cricket matches with military teams were the only games which it seemed fitting for local clubs to engage in'.

To that end, in 1917 Eastleigh Athletic CC entertained players from a local ASC Remount Depot. 'Soldiers in training or stationed away from their homes need a little recreation and friendly conversation.' Mr WG Willoughby took a team from Eastleigh to oppose an XI from the Royal Victoria Hospital, Netley, winning 124 to 102. The Rest Camp Second XI team based on the Common at Southampton was advertising in the press for teams who could arrange fixtures in the area. In one match, against Invicta CC, note was made of the 'very friendly and sporting spirit shown' by the local clubs, who 'play cricket in every sense of the word'. A Royal Garrison Artillery (Siege Artillery Signalling Depot) side was invited to the County Ground, Southampton, to play Jesse Hopkins' XII (Hants Club and Ground). Phil Mead, the prolific Hampshire and England batsman, appeared for the club side. On this occasion, his bowling was more to the fore as he took 6-33. Such was the concentration of troops in the Southampton area that an

Artillery Cricket Competition was organised between the four companies, with the winning team awarded a shield. The matches took place at the County Ground. A collection was taken for the Royal South Hants and Southampton Hospital.

The opening matches of Southampton's War Cricket League were played on 4 May 1915, with 15 clubs split over two divisions. Prominent local cricketing worthies had given the competition their patronage and blessing. The two-division league included teams from Harland and Wolff Eastleigh Mechanical Engineers, and Northam Ironworks. Concern was expressed in a letter to the *Hampshire Advertiser* about the expansion of informal Sunday evening cricket in the area. The correspondent, self-styled 'a Friend to Social Order', complained the players and bystanders were 'ill-employed' and 'scurrilous language … quarrelling and gambling' was the result. On the surface the knockabout cricketing gatherings were 'apparently free from mischief' but were, evidently, 'full of evil'.

Hampshire's 1917 annual report sombrely stated 'several of the Hampshire players have fallen in the war'. By the time of the club's annual meeting in November, however, thoughts were turning to the post-war livelihood of professional cricketers. Dr Russell Bencraft, who held several leading positions at the club across many years of service, thought it wrong that fit and healthy men could earn a good wage during the summer but do no work at all through the winter. Thus, schemes to encourage the winter employment of cricketers should be considered. However, in contrast to other clubs, the war years proved to be beneficial financially, if not on the playing side, with the club's debt nearly halving from £489 to £252. By 1917 the club had paid off its overdraft due to the generosity of members continuing to subscribe in the absence of on-field action.

Convalescing soldiers enjoyed the psychologically calming effects of white flannel-clad cricketers flitting across Britain's emerald-coloured fields. Over 1,000 wounded warriors enjoyed a match between XIs of the Southampton and Portsmouth Corporations, played at Hampshire's County Ground in early August. Special travel arrangements were in place to transport them by road and rail from across Hampshire and Sussex.

In all, 24 men who had played first-class cricket for the county before the war had lost their lives. Hampshire cricket needed rebuilding from scratch. All available manpower was called upon. Forty-nine-year-old Ledger

Hill, who had played for the county against Billy Murdoch's 1890 Australians, was included in the team to face the AIF XI. Hill's Test record is remarkable, a batting average of 62.75 and a bowling average of 2 for his four wickets, from his three matches in South Africa in 1895/96.

Also in the Hampshire side to face the AIF XI was Dallas Brooks, a 22-year-old all-rounder who had been wounded at Gallipoli and won the DSO. He had been half blown up when one of the makeshift jam tin bomb catapults invented in the trenches failed. Little did anyone know on this day that Brooks would eventually, as Lieutenant-General Sir Dallas Brooks, serve as Governor of Victoria.

Southampton had enjoyed 48 rain-free days before the Australians came to town. Sadly, the first day was washed out, making the match a two-day affair. The hosts made 191 in their first innings, with Phil Mead making 91. The AIF made 136 all out in reply, saved from total embarrassment by a Trenerry half-ton, while Alec Kennedy claimed 6-56 for the locals. Hampshire then played out the remaining 14 overs as the match ended in an inevitable draw. English weather to the rescue once again, leaving the AIF XI still undefeated.

Chapter 13

Gentlemen of England

Lord's Cricket Ground, St John's Wood on 23–25 June 1919
Result: Gentlemen of England won by an innings and 133 runs

WITH ITS roots in the early 19th century, the 274 Gentlemen v Players contests which took place until the abolition of the cricketing class distinction in 1963 aroused keen interest in English cricket circles. For Harry Altham, the 1860s, 70s and 80s were the halcyon days of amateur cricket, as the public schools and universities churned out famous cricketers. Ironically, much of the success of the Gentlemen in that period – 27 wins and only five defeats – was down to the non-public-school-educated WG Grace. Grace typified much of the class snobbery which bifurcated cricketers between amateurs and professionals.

Amateurs frequently received lavish expenses for giving up their time to play cricket, whilst professionals were kept on a tight leash by their county clubs. Unacceptable behaviour, such as Yorkshire professional Bobby Peel's historically disputed on-field intoxication in 1897, could lead to a player's livelihood being taken away from him. Amateurs were given more latitude. With the rise of county cricket in the decades approaching the Great War, the pendulum began to swing back as professionals such as Jack Hobbs and Wilfred Rhodes ensured a tough challenge to the Gentlemen.

In their third Lord's appearance of the tour, the Australians at last met with defeat, the Gentlemen winning in uncompromising fashion by an innings and 133 runs. Though a little rain fell late on the first afternoon there was nothing in the condition of the ground to account for the one-sided result. *Wisden* continued:

> One may safely say that the Gentlemen were the better side, but whereas they were at the top of their form at every point, the Australians for once lost all their fighting spirit. The Gentlemen's victory was made certain on the second day when Douglas

> and Falcon, by means of really wonderful bowling, got the Australians out in two hours.

It is unknown why a match was arranged for the AIF XI versus the Gentlemen of England, but not the Players – although one can speculate a connection to the enmity between the leagues and counties outlined in the previous chapters. When the amateurs took on the professionals at Lord's in September 1919 they were roundly thumped by an innings and 110 runs. Nevertheless, when the MCC Committee met on 16 June, amongst those invited to play were: Plum Warner, Johnny Douglas, Hon. Clarence Bruce, Michael Falcon, 'Father' Marriott, 'Farmer' White, and the Rev. Frank Gillingham. Here was the English governing class in its representative splendour – the original Mr Cricket in the shape of Warner; the Olympic boxer and all-round sporting hero in Johnny Douglas representing the aesthetic and manly qualities required of Britain's elite; and representatives of the Tory Party, the aristocracy, Church of England, the military and agriculture. Indeed, the *Sunday Mirror* report on the match referred to 'Commander Evans', 'Major Douglas' and 'Captain Warner'.

At the close of the first day's play, the amateurs had hit up 378/6. Frank Gillingham had 'seldom played better cricket' according to the *Sheffield Independent* as 'Merry Hitting' was seen at Lord's. Despite Collins setting a deep field for the churchman, Gillingham managed to force the ball to the boundary on several occasions in his 83.

With Johnny Douglas his usual obdurate self, most of the Gentlemen got a start. The *Wisden* report noted Nottinghamshire's Arthur Carr, 'after a rather shaky start, drove Gregory's fast bowling with refreshing vigour'. Vigour towards the greater cause was what the old Etonian had displayed upon receiving a telegram whilst batting against Surrey at The Oval on 4 August 1914. 'I'll have one more over,' he is reputed to have said, before throwing his wicket away. Carr would play a pivotal role in future Anglo-Australian cricket relations as the man who primed Harold Larwood and Bill Voce to hone the art of fast leg-theory bowling when captain of Nottinghamshire in the early 1930s. The bonhomie of 1919 gave way to the bodyline furore of 1932/33.

By the end of the second day's play, seen by 2,717 paying customers as well as MCC members, the Gentlemen 'had the game in their hands' as the Australians needed a further 168 runs to avert an innings defeat, with only two wickets remaining. The Australian first innings 'came as a surprise' as 'there seemed nothing to stand in the way of good scoring'. Eighty-five all out was a poor showing by the AIF XI; 149/8 by the close of play was slightly better, but not enough to make a contest of it.

The *Wisden* match report recorded:

> Falcon made the ball swerve in deadly fashion, and Douglas had a little swerve to help his irreproachable length. Against the two the Australians were helpless, and though their batting was better in the follow-on there never seemed the slightest chance of avoiding defeat.

Michael Falcon never played in the County Championship, his 89 first-class appearances coming mainly for Cambridge University. He played Minor Counties cricket for Norfolk for several years, captaining the club for 34 years, a period which spanned both world wars. At the time he ran through the Australian batting, he was Michael Falcon MP, having been elected in 1918 as the member for East Norfolk. Falcon seemed to rather enjoy playing against Australians, claiming another six-for for Archie MacLaren's XI which famously inflicted the only defeat on Warwick Armstrong's 1921 tourists.

It took the 12th match of the tour for the Australians to be on the wrong end of the result, going down by an innings. The comprehensive victory meted out to the AIF XI by the Gentlemen of England at Lord's was greeted with joy by MCC members and those who treasured the supposed dash and flair of amateur cricketers. For *Wisden*, it was 'the most important match of the whole programme'. This was despite the fact that, man-for-man, the scratch XI that was got together by CI Thornton for the Scarborough Festival match at the end of the tour was of superior calibre.

Collins had stated he hoped the Australians could achieve some manner of retribution by taking on a team of Test quality at the Scarborough fixture. This keenness was brought into sharper focus by the decision of MCC not to send a touring party down under in 1919-20. For the Australians, the Ashes were never far from their thoughts. 'Nip' Pellew pinched a stump from the ground at the end of the match and it was suggested that he burn it to create an army Ashes.

Chapter 14

Northamptonshire

County Ground, Northampton on 26–28 June 1919
Result: Australian Imperial Forces won by 196 runs

THE DECLARATION of war in 1914 had had an immediate impact on Northamptonshire CCC. A team was not sent to Taunton to play the fixture arranged against Somerset. The club, which had joined the County Championship as recently as 1905, had finished runners-up in the 1912 competition and looked destined to become a strong force in English cricket.

Behind this façade lay deep problems. An Extraordinary General Meeting in November 1914 reported heavy financial losses, and winter retainers for the professionals were scrapped. It was hoped a combination of continuing subscriptions from members and a lack of cricket in 1915 would be a boon to club finances. One attendee, Dr Ross, opined it would be wrong to play next year when men were wanted at the front. 'The continuance of football was a sorry exhibition,' he stated. The County Ground was turned over for use by military cricketers.

The expected financial upturn in 1915 did not materialise. By the autumn the club owed nearly £1,200 to creditors and had a bank overdraft of nearly £1,500 against assets of just over £700. War also ravaged Northamptonshire's playing resources.

Absent from the Northamptonshire side which faced the Australians were the three Denton brothers. Billy, Jack and Don had all played in a match against Sussex at Hove in July 1914. One source described the trio as 'not only consistently effective, but wonderfully versatile in their utterly different styles'. Playing as amateurs, dividing their time between cricket and an archetypal Northamptonshire family bootmaking business, the brothers had potentially promising careers in front of them. That high summer excursion to Hove had resulted in an opening partnership of 145 between twins Billy and Jack before Don, coming in at No. 7, made 51 not out on his first-class debut.

In May 1918, Lieutenants Jack and Billy Denton had been reported missing. As identical as the Bedser twins (born just a month later), the Dentons' wartime experiences set a similar pattern of inseparability that the famous Surrey duo were to follow in the later war. The officers had joined the West Kent Regiment together, transferred to the Northamptonshire Regiment simultaneously and obtained their commissions at the same time. Thankfully, the Denton twins' father received news a week later confirming both his boys had been taken prisoner. They spent the rest of the war in an island PoW camp in the Baltic and made a safe return via Denmark in early 1919.

Their younger brother was not so fortunate. Don Denton had his leg amputated above the knee in 1917 as a result of war wounds. Remarkably, the stoic Don played three first-class matches after the war, with one of his brothers acting as a runner. Opposing captains were more than happy to allow for this diversion from the Laws of Cricket, one stating, 'If any fellow has been to the war and has had his leg off and wants to play, he is good enough for me and can have twenty runners.' In his final first-class match Don made 15 and 37, *The Times* lamenting of his seven-match first-class career:

'One can only sigh and wonder what he might have done but for his handicap.'

Another Northamptonshire cricketer reported missing, Private Sidney King, who played in four matches for the county in 1907 and 1908, wrote to his wife at Rushden to relay that he was safe and well as a prisoner of war. A similar deliverance befell Mark Cox, who had played in the club's inaugural first-class match in 1905. Their team-mate, George Thompson, fell seriously ill the same year and spent a long period of convalescence in the vast Netley Hospital by the Solent. His osteomyelitis left him unable to walk without sticks during 1919 and 1920. When he resumed playing in 1921 he was never the same bowler as he had been previously.

In August 1918, William 'Bumper' Wells, the Daventry hard-hitting batsman and fast bowler, was gassed and invalided back to England for treatment at Duston War Hospital in Northampton. He recovered to re-establish his place in the team throughout the early 1920s. However, Northampton's pre-war captain and pre-eminent batsman, Sydney Smith, had migrated to New Zealand, never to return to Northamptonshire's ranks.[29]

---

29 No relation to the Australian Board of Control chairman.

Despite playing and financial losses, Northamptonshire CCC decided to soldier on in 1919, playing a basic 12 Championship matches as well as the AIF fixture. *Wisden* described the programme as 'being as good as could be expected in the circumstances'. The club would subside from being title contenders before the war to perennial underdogs and frequent 17th finishers between the world wars. 1919 was not such a bad year, with two victories, four defeats (two to the mighty Yorkshire) and six draws.

The team Northamptonshire put out into the field was one of the weakest first-class outfits the AIF XI faced. Five of the players would play but a handful of matches for the county and none of the side won Test match honours.

One debutant who would have a long-term impact on Northamptonshire cricket was fast bowler Albert Thomas. The Welshman had been billeted in Northampton with the Welsh Regiment, thus fulfilling a new residential qualification criterion for county eligibility. Thomas was on leave from service in Russia, as the British government sought to crush the new Bolshevik state. Thomas had attracted the attention of groundsman Alf Stockwin when he came to bowl in the nets at Wantage Road in the war. After an unsuccessful debut against the AIF XI, Thomas was taken on by Northampton Grammar School as a coach and groundsman so the county club could keep an eye on his progress. He justified the club's interest with figures of 9-30 against the mighty Yorkshire in 1920 and became a fixture in the side. He would go on to play 288 matches, taking an impressive 832 wickets at 25.52.

While the match was being played out the newspapers were full of the news coming from Paris that a peace treaty had been signed at the Palace of Versailles. Former England captain HDG 'Shrimp' Leveson Gower attended the peace conference in his role as liaison officer between the War Office and the Foreign Office. The role, he recalled, 'appeared to consist largely in arranging for a supply of cars for politicians and officials at the Conference'.

Despite the match falling during the height of summer, the *Northampton Chronicle and Echo* described the weather as 'more suited to football than to cricket'. A cold wind made watching the match anything but pleasant, with a small attendance on day one. Just 800 spectators paid for admission. 'Taffy' Thomas's Northamptonshire debut was inauspicious, with 22 runs being conceded from his first five overs. Herbie Collins was dismissed in freakish circumstances. Attempting to hit a bad ball to the leg boundary, the Australian captain caught it on the shoulder of his bat and played it into his face, from whence it went to the hands of Hawes at first slip. A century from Jack Gregory, who was opening the batting, was the mainstay of the AIF's 297 all out.

Northamptonshire began their reply well, reaching 100 for the loss of two wickets by the end of day one.

By the end of the second day's play, the AIF had a lead of 228 with four wickets in hand in their second innings. 'If we can get them out for another 50 we shall have a chance of winning,' one Northamptonshire player was quoted as saying. However, the final four AIF wickets were good for another 137. Set 366 to win, the task proved too much for the home side.

The eventual margin of the AIF XI victory, 186 runs, reflected credit both on the fighting qualities of the makeshift Northamptonshire side and 'the way in which the Australians worked to win'.

Hampshire CCC Roll of Honour *[p.19]* Image courtesy of Dave Allen

'The Sterner Game' poem by Scottish sport journalist Leo Munro [p.30]

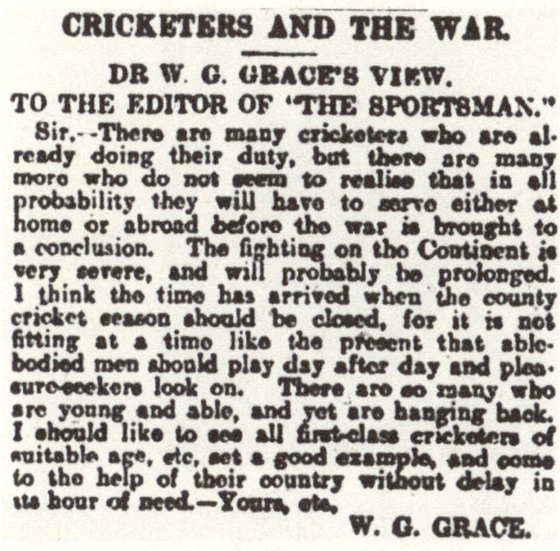

CRICKETERS AND THE WAR.

DR W. G. GRACE'S VIEW.

TO THE EDITOR OF "THE SPORTSMAN."

Sir,—There are many cricketers who are already doing their duty, but there are many more who do not seem to realise that in all probability they will have to serve either at home or abroad before the war is brought to a conclusion. The fighting on the Continent is very severe, and will probably be prolonged. I think the time has arrived when the county cricket season should be closed, for it is not fitting at a time like the present that able-bodied men should play day after day and pleasure-seekers look on. There are so many who are young and able, and yet are hanging back. I should like to see all first-class cricketers of suitable age, etc, set a good example, and come to the help of their country without delay in its hour of need.—Yours, etc,

W. G. GRACE.

The Grand Old Man of cricket has his say [p.31]

Jack Davis AKA Not Out [p.35]

PF 'Plum' Warner [p.41]

Army XI v AIF XI in aid of St Dunstan's [p.46]

ARMY CRICKET MATCH.

ENGLAND V. AUSTRALIA.

LONDON, Saturday.

Unique interest was taken in the army cricket game at Lord's. where a great crowd witnessed the season's foremost fixture. The weather for several days had been fine and hot, and today it was brilliant, with a fast wicket. The teams were:—

Australia.—Barbour (captain), P. Docker, C. Docker, Kelleway, Macartney (New South Wales), Matthews, N. Dean (Victoria), Stirling, W. Munday. G. Inkster (South Australia), M'Andrews (Queensland).

England.—Warner (captain), Douglas, Fender, N. Knox, Blythe, E. Tyldesley, E. Hendren, D. Jennings, W. Franklin, Makepeace, and Lee (Middlesex).

Army cricket match at Lord's, 1917 *[p.46]*

At an auction, cricket mementoes raised £90. Scores:—

AUSTRALIANS.

KELLEWAY, b Knox	53
MACARTNEY, lbw., b Douglas	0
MUNDAY. c Lee, b Blythe	5
BARBOUR, c Hendren, b Lee	30
P. DOCKER, lbw., b Lee	1
STIRLING, run out	7
MATTHEWS, c Fradklin, b Knox	1
C. DOCKER, st. Franklin, b Lee	13
DEAN, b Lee	8
INKSTER, not out	4
M'ANDREWS, b Lee	0
Extras	6
Total	130

Bowling.—Lee 5 for 22; Knox, 2 for 34; Blythe, 1 for 16; Douglas, 1 for 39; Fender, 1 for 12.

ENGLAND.

MAKEPEACE, c Inkster, b C. Docker	13
LEE, b Macartney	7
TYLDESLEY, c C. Docker, b Andrews	38
WARNER, st Inkster, b Macartney	34
DOUGLAS, b C. Docker	20
HENDREN, c Inkster, b Macartney	8
JENNINGS, c Barbour, b Matthews	26
FENDER, c Barbour, b C. Docker	5
KNOX, c Macartney, b Barbour	6
BLYTHE, not out	2
FRANKLIN, absent	0
Extras	11
Total	162

Bowling: C. Docker, 3 for 16; Macartney, 3 for 34; Barbour, 1 for 15; Matthews, 1 for 32; M'Andrews, 1 for 29; Kelleway, none for 17; Stirling, none for 9.

Lord's Army match scorecard *[p.46]*

(Left) Dominions captain EP Barbour greets the King *[p.49]*

(Right) Taylor almost caught *[p.56]*

INDIAN GYMKHANA CLUB

C. H. Gunasekara, c Taylor, b Matthews	6
Cadet K. S. Hamatsinhji, c Barbour, b M'Andrew	6
P. Saravanamattu, b Matthews	6
M. P. Bajana, c Willis, b M'Andrew	16
P. Subbarrayan, c M'Andrew, b Matthews	0
A. C. Wijayaratne, b Docker	6
K. S. Pratapsinhji, b Matthews	0
G. W. Karunaratna, c and b Matthews	1
J. L. Kotelawala, b Matthews	6
E. D. Carolis, not out	0
R. J. Tata, b Matthews	0
B 4, lb 6	10
Total	57

Second Innings.

Hamatsinhji, b Barbour	2
Saravanamattu, run out	2
Subbarrayan, not out	4
Pratapsinhji, b Kelleway	3
Tata, b Kelleway	8
Extras	3
Total (four wickets)	22

AUSTRALIAN XI.

Lieut. C. Kelleway (N.S.W.), b Gunasekara	2
Capt. E. P. Barbour (N.S.W.), (capt), b Gunasekara	2
L.-Cpl. W. Sewart (Vic.), b Tata	23
Gnr. J. Taylor (N.S.W.), b Tata	7
Gnr. A. W. Lampard (Vic.), b Gunasekara	15
Lieut. C. B. Willis (Vic.), c Pratapsinhji, b Gunasekara	31
Sgt. W. Stirling (S.A.), b Tata	0
Pte. J. T. Matthews (Vic.), b Gunasekara	0
Lieut. C. T. Docker (N.S.W.), c Bajana, b Tata	0
Cpl. G. B. Inkster (Adelaide), b Tata	9
Pte. W. M'Andrew (Queensland), not out	0
B. 7, L. B. 5	12
Total	105

BOWLING ANALYSIS.

Indian Gymkhana.—First Innings: Docker, 14 overs, 7 maidens, 10 runs, 1 wicket; Kelle-

Lord's Army match scorecard *[p.48]*

The King meeting with Lord Hawke and Walter Long *[p.57*

Long narrowly avoids a run-out [p.58]

Gordon Campbell recruits for the Sportsmen's Battalion [p.66]

Tibby Cotter in 1905 [p.70]

Frank Iredale [p.25]

An AIF team at Tidworth in 1916 featuring both Barbour and Lewis; Barbour would have been the captain on this occasion. Short Stop AKA Billy Stewart is standing on the far right. [p.105]

Dorothy Brunton, hostess of 'The Digger's Rest' [p.104]

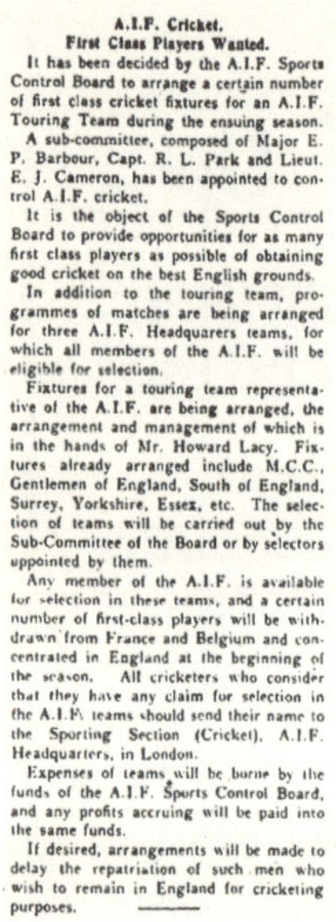

A.I.F. Cricket.
First Class Players Wanted.

It has been decided by the A.I.F. Sports Control Board to arrange a certain number of first class cricket fixtures for an A.I.F. Touring Team during the ensuing season.

A sub-committee, composed of Major E. P. Barbour, Capt. R. L. Park and Lieut. E. J. Cameron, has been appointed to control A.I.F. cricket.

It is the object of the Sports Control Board to provide opportunities for as many first class players as possible of obtaining good cricket on the best English grounds.

In addition to the touring team, programmes of matches are being arranged for three A.I.F. Headquarers teams, for which all members of the A.I.F. will be eligible for selection.

Fixtures for a touring team representative of the A.I.F. are being arranged, the arrangement and management of which is in the hands of Mr. Howard Lacy. Fixtures already arranged include M.C.C., Gentlemen of England, South of England, Surrey, Yorkshire, Essex, etc. The selection of teams will be carried out by the Sub-Committee of the Board or by selectors uppointed by them.

Any member of the A.I.F. is available for selection in these teams, and a certain number of first-class players will be withdrawn from France and Belgium and concentrated in England at the beginning of the season. All cricketers who consider that they have any claim for selection in the A.I.F. teams should send their name to the Sporting Section (Cricket), A.I.F. Headquarters, in London.

Expenses of teams will be borne by the funds of the A.I.F. Sports Control Board, and any profits accruing will be paid into the same funds.

If desired, arrangements will be made to delay the repatriation of such men who wish to remain in England for cricketing purposes.

Appeal for AIF Cricketers [p.106]

The cricketing Gregory family [p.108]

Hammy Love [p.114]

The AIF XI

The AIF 'XI' take the field against LG Robinson's 'XI' [p.112]

Cricket at Old Buckenham, Norfolk [p.112]

Frank Gillingham [p.120]

Church v Australians (Clergy v AIF HQ)

Johnny Douglas in 1906 [p.124]

'Young Jack' Hearne in 1922 [p.140]

Ed Long and Nip Pellew [p.137]

Carl Willis and Bert Oldfield [p.148]

Strudwick and Smith in the munitions factory [p.156]

George Robey in 'Zig Zag' 1918 [p.175]

Surrey cricketers playing golf before a day of munitions work *[p.160]*

George Hirst *[p.188]*

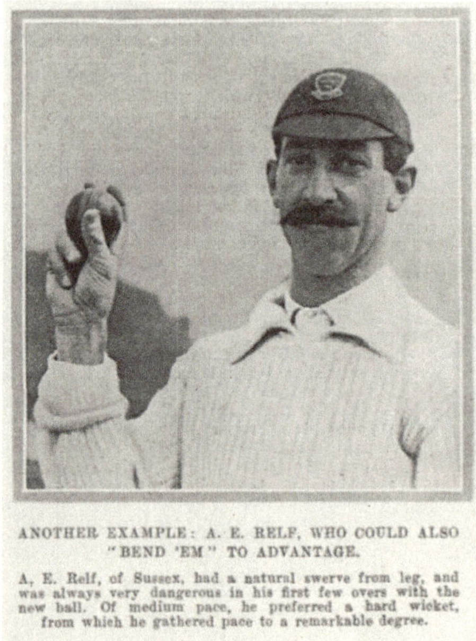

Albert Relf *[p.262]*

Lampard and Stirling *[p.186]*

AIF XI take to the field at Bramall Lane *[p.188]*

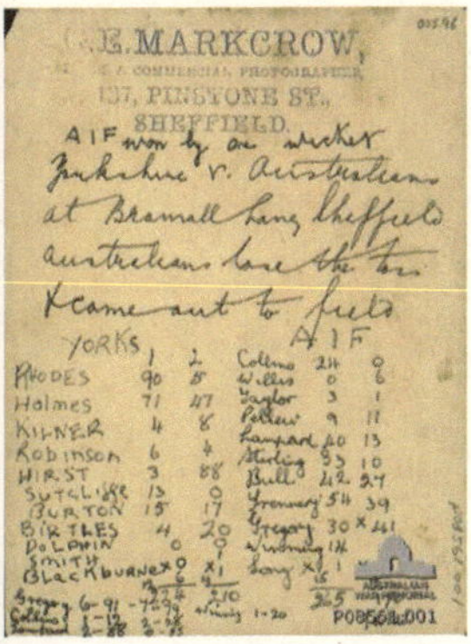

An impromptu spectator scorecard of the Yorkshire Match [p.188]

JJ Booth [p.192]

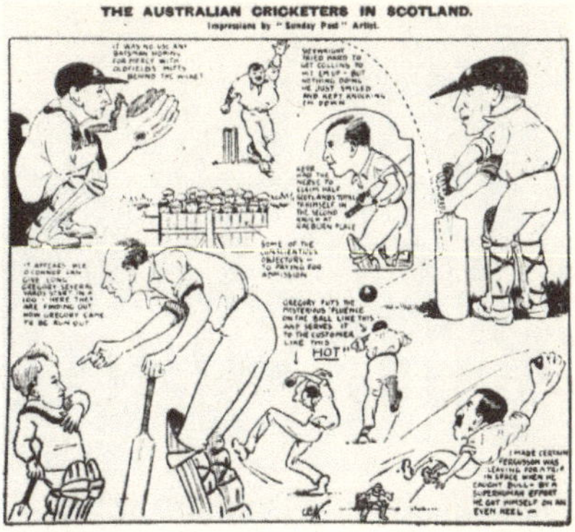

Australian Cricketers in Scotland [p.230]

L-R: Captain Collins (off camera), Captain Docker, Mr Dawson, Captain Long and Captain Trenerry. [p.231]

The AIF Eight train for the Henley Regatta [p.234]

Leach (or Gamage) Catapault [p.244]

Bill Trenerry [p.244]

HK Foster [p.247]

Johnny Taylor [p.249]

(Left) Winning and Trenerry [p.256]

(Right) Docker and Gregory [p.263]

The 1920/21 English team at St Peter's College, Adelaide. [p.273]

(L-R) JR Mason, DW Carr, HL Simms, GL Jessop, JWHT Douglas, GA Faulkner [p.292]

The poster for the final match of the tour. Note Lacy's name is misspelt. [p.300]

Signed dinner card – 15 September 1919 [p.303]

HMT Ascanius [p.307]

HMT Aeneas [p.236]

Hilda Hope McMaugh [p.328]

Chapter 15

The First Scottish Tour

Shawholm, Glasgow on 30 June–1 July 1919
Result: Australian Imperial Forces won by an innings and 560 runs

Raeburn Place, Edinburgh on 2–3 July
Result: Match drawn

Hamilton Crescent, Glasgow on 4–5 July 1919
Result: Match drawn

THE SCOTTISH leg of Australian tours first entered the itinerary with Joe Darling's 1902 side. Although the quality of play was far from the English standard, the public support was similar to that in England outside the powerhouse counties. As many as 8,000 showed up to see the AIF XI play the West of Scotland on the first day of a whirlwind tour. The Scottish schedule highlights how hard the players were working – this was far from a relaxed social excursion. A train from Northampton to Glasgow on the morning of 30 June, a two-day match against West of Scotland starting that afternoon which lasted almost to the final minute; the morning train to Edinburgh for another two-day match against Scotland on 2–3 July which they arrived late for – before again taking the morning train back across to Glasgow for another two-day match on 4–5 July.

The first match almost coming out a draw belies the actual scoreline – these were two-day matches after all. In the sole Australian innings only Pellew and Gregory failed. The usually reliable batsmen added just 18 and 10 runs respectively. The next lowest score was Taylor's 75, followed by Collins' 94. Trenerry, Bull, Stirling and Murray all scored centuries, the latter top-scoring with 150. West of Scotland did one better however, with all five bowlers scoring the more inglorious of cricket's centuries.

At 733/6 Collins sent the hapless Scots into bat, being already in to the second and final day of play. Mathie-Morton's 25 was the highlight. Docker, Collins, and the sub O'Connor all took three wickets for under 30 runs. With the entire Scottish order bundled out for 85, the only thing to do was send them back in. Eighty-eight was all West of Scotland could manage, with Gregory being the chief destroyer with four wickets, the Australians snatching victory from the jaws of a light-induced draw.

Scotland won the toss in Edinburgh and went in for a bat. James Sorrie joined Scottish legend John Kerr – one of the initial inductees into the Scottish cricket hall of fame and still the longest-serving Scottish national player – for a more than respectable first-wicket partnership of 64. Kerr went for 45, and the score was soon 65/3, but Sorrie held on to score 79, including an impressive 96-run fifth-wicket partnership with future president of the Scottish Cricket Union, Gilbert Hole. With Sorrie out, Hole held on with a tail collapsing under the weight of a lightning Gregory spell to score 67, setting a reasonable total for the hosts of 266.

The Australian response was far from authoritative. Groves, and particularly Sievwright bowled tightly for Scotland, taking seven wickets between them. Most of the Australian order could get a start, but none could go on to a big score, most getting out trying to move the scoreboard on. The hapless substitute O'Connor ran out the all-conquering Gregory (perhaps part of the reason he would not feature in another match on the tour). It was only captain Collins' mammoth 159 that handed the Australians a 94-run first-innings lead.

However, by now it was well into the second – and final – day of play. All the Scots had to do was hold on and they would go away with a draw. Standing in the Caledonians' way was Gregory. The 'Streak' matched his six wickets in the first innings, this time for just 38 runs. However, Kerr stood like a rock. The opener was still standing on 40 not out when bad light stopped play with the Scots floundering at 79/8.

The final match of the first Scottish tour was much the same story. Collins won the toss and chose to bat. At 91/4 the home side must have felt in with a sniff. So too when 155/5 turned into 156/7 not long before rain halted play on day one. However, half centuries from Bull and Docker batting at nine and ten, supported by a stalwart 27 not out from Oldfield, set the Scots a first-innings target of 357, with not much daylight left to play. The Scots struggled to a first-innings total of 113 and the match was called a draw with no prospect of a result.

However, there was little respite for the players. The following day was Sunday, a day of rest for the players, to be spent on the train heading south to West Hartlepool for the match against Durham on Monday.

Eric Bull was initially rejected from the AIF on medical grounds in 1915. He did not let this deter his war effort, however, and he joined Austin Diamond's promotional side for the Sportsman's 1000 who played various games in Australia to encourage young men to sign up for the war. With the slackening of enlistment standards, he made it into the AIF in late 1916, leaving for the front in mid-1917. At the stop at Fremantle on the way over he missed the ship, or in the words of the official documents was 'inadvertently left at Fremantle' and had to wait for the next transport to the front, earning him a demotion. Although he had played a handful of matches for New South Wales prior to the war and was a member of the Australian version of I Zingari after, the AIF XI tour was to be the bulk, and end of, his first-class cricketing career.

Chapter 16

Durham and Leicester

Other Sports

It is worth taking a moment to consider what the public mood was at the time. It was not just up to the cricketers of the AIF to provide the boost to the sporting public and rejuvenate the hopes of the nation. Everywhere one looked there were signs of life returning to normal – especially on the sporting field – and that a new and exciting future was imminent. The weather of the gentle English summer had turned fine, giant crowds turning out for any piece of excitement.

In mid-June the first successful trans-Atlantic flight was completed by Alcock and Brown. This was followed on 2 July by the first return flight by rigid airship, beginning the age of commercial air transport. On 28 June – five years to the day after the assassination of the Archduke – the Treaty of Versailles was signed, followed on 4 July by massive US Independence Day celebrations in London, where tens of thousands of Englishmen waved the Stars and Stripes to give thanks to their American cousins. On the 6th a large outdoor 'thanksgiving service' was held at St Paul's Cathedral, the press commenting, 'Never before has St Paul's Cathedral been so thronged with notable people,' including the King and Queen, Prince Albert and Princess Mary, 15,000 servicemen and an uncountable number of the general public.

The county cricket season was in full swing, the crowds returning in greater than pre-war numbers. So too the crowds returned to the first full English horse racing season since the outbreak of the war. The icing on the racing cake was Galloper Light winning the Paris Grand Prix, the first time in 13 years an English horse had taken France's greatest race (the first Prix de l'Arc de Triomphe, now considered the biggest prize in French racing would begin the following year).

From 22 June to 6 July the Inter-Allied Games were held in Paris. Around 1,500 soldier-athletes from 18 Allied nations competed in 19 sports, largely of the Olympic variety, but with the notable inclusion of hand grenade throwing, a distance rather than accuracy-based event. It was won by Fred Thomson of the USA with a throw of 74.93m. Fred would go on after the war to become one of the most popular actors in the silent cowboy film genre. With most Commonwealth athletes already repatriated at least back to England, the Games were dominated by French and especially American athletes; a fact highlighted by the entrance list for rugby union featuring only French, American and Romanian teams. Free tickets and widespread public information campaigns ensured large attendances and the Games provided a significant 'fillip' to the French public.

6 July saw the return of competitive rowing with the 'Henley Peace Regatta'. This special event was organised to allow those involved in 'menial' labour – banned at the regatta until 1937 – to compete. This was essentially to allow for an AIF team to enter, and because the organising committee – reflecting the concerns in cricket – felt it too soon to begin serious competition. The AIF beat the Oxford crew by a length, winning the King's Cup, which became the annual prize for the champion state in men's eights at the Australian Rowing Championships.

Finally, late June had seen the return of Wimbledon – and the natural order of tennis. The finals, played out while the Australians were at Durham, were dominated by Australian men. The men's singles and doubles finals were all-Australian affairs, while a fifth Australian was the male half of the successful mixed doubles champions. The women's tournament was a story of three women – Frenchwoman Suzanne Lenglen, American Elizabeth Ryan and Brit Dorothea Lambert Chambers. Unfortunately for the home crowd Lambert Chambers lost the women's singles, doubles and mixed doubles finals.

Durham and Leicester

Park Drive, West Hartlepool on 7–8 July 1919
Result: Match drawn
Aylestone Road, Leicester on 11–12 July 1919
Result: Match drawn

The AIF were back in England, but not yet back to big matches. The non-first-class match against minor county Durham was advantage Australia at stumps on day one, ahead by 421 runs with two wickets and Durham's second innings still to come. But the locals were playing better than the scoreline suggests. Most notable was Thomas Kinch's 105 – the top score for the match. For the AIF it was a whole team effort, with no individual standing out.

The match against Leicestershire likewise ended in a draw. However, it was not advantage Australia, it was game, set, **checks watch** why are the Australians still batting? In the two-day match, the Australians had obviously decided to make hay while the sun shone. Collins, Pellew and Willis had field days. Collins got his 121 out of the way in two and a half hours – decent pace for the time. But it was Pellew and Willis's 276-run partnership that was the highlight of the match. Willis ending the innings on 156 not out, while Pellew fell 13 runs short of the tour's first double ton. The AIF declared overnight, five wickets down for 551 runs. In response Leicester made what in other matches would have been a respectable total of 224, but by then the day was almost within an hour of stumps, allowing Murray and Bull to carefully block out the draw.

Leicestershire were one of the sides erring on the side of experience in these first tentative days back at cricket. Four of the strongest players in the side – Cecil Wood, Harry Whitehead, John King and Samuel Coe – had been playing first-class cricket since the previous century. Although arguably the best player in the side, George Geary was at the beginning of a career that would feature 14 Tests in which he took 46 wickets, including four five-wicket hauls.

In his 549 games for Leicestershire between 1912 and 1938 he took 2,063 wickets, including 100 or more in a season 11 times, including his record season in 1929 when he took 152 wickets at an average of 19.59. That year he took his best first-class figures of 10-18 against Glamorgan. He also nearly did the 100 wicket/1,000 run double that season, scoring his career best of 923. While serving in the Royal Flying Corps early on in the war he had an incident with an aircraft propeller resulting in injuries to his left shoulder and thigh that were still bothering him, making 1919 his third-worst season.

Carl Willis

Carl Bleakley Willis was an up-and-coming sportsman at the outbreak of the war, playing first-class cricket for Victoria, in the Victorian Football League for University and South Melbourne, and rowing for the Mercantile Club, all while being the cricket writer for *The Winner*. Willis was one of the few voices calling for a continuation of cricket when the war broke out, arguing those who can fight should go and fight, but those who cannot should not be denied sport, suggesting it would lead to excessive alcohol abuse.

On enlistment he was allocated to the Australian Pioneers Battalion, a unit made up of skilled tradesmen. The officer in charge wanted athletes who 'could handle the strain' he expected from his men. Upon arrival in England, he was first stationed at Salisbury Plains where he found some time for cricket: 'I have had a couple of games of cricket here but was very much astray on both occasions. There are a large number of old sporting fellows round here'. His letters home provide insights into the day-to-day life of the soldier, especially while on leave in London (assumedly these letters made it through the censors more often than details from the front). He wrote of 'trying to buy a policeman' in London, the experience of which he describes:

> Many times had we read and heard of his manifold qualities, and he does deserve every word said in his praise. He more than fulfilled our highest expectations. He was an inquiry office constantly, our guide and general guardian; he seemed to be quite

> pleased to direct us; in fact, he could not possibly have been more decent. In fact, I think the proper way to describe him is as a human directory.

In another letter he speaks of walking the London streets at night:

> London at night with the lights dimmed. Well, it is bad enough in the daytime when you can see, but at night – hopeless. Had it not been for the policeman and an occasional taxi driver we would have wandered the streets all night.
>
> One of the fellows with us got off a bus fifty yards from our hotel; he walked and walked for over an hour. At last, in desperation he gave a boy sixpence to lead him home, and found then that he was only about twenty yards away.

He played in some of the matches at Tidworth in 1917, writing of them:

> It reminds one sadly of old times to play cricket in the morning, and then for both teams to sit down in flannels to a nicely served lunch, and then play again in the afternoon. The only trouble I can find with regard to the matches we have played is that one does not like going back to camp life again. The contrast is rather too strong.

Willis was also possibly involved in the invention of a unique form of fishing:

> I struck an example here of the difference between the Tommies and our fellows. There is one of the many little streams that irrigate the country and run into the main canals flowing quietly along just near the camp. Some Tommies found fish in it, borrowed an old net from civilians, mended it, and tried to drag the stream. Next evening our fellows arrive there with Mills Grenades and fished with them. There is no doubt about it, they are the best bait I have ever seen Dozens of fish came up stunned. When the whole

> thing was finished, much to our disgust, the fish weren't much good to eat, they were very bony, and tasted of mud.

However, it is perhaps his reflections on the war itself that are most valuable:

> I don't care who the man is writing he cannot on paper show the reality of the thing. Again I have used a wrong word – reality – there is no such thing as realness, everything is unreal much the same as a dream or trance.

On returning home from the war, Willis returned to the South Melbourne Football Club as captain and played cricket with Victoria until 1928. He was selected for the non-Test tour of New Zealand in 1920/21 but was unable to join the side. He died in 1930 due to complications from the injuries he received in the war.

Chapter 17

Derbyshire, HK Foster's XI, Worcestershire

County Ground, Derby on 14–15 July 1919
Result: Derbyshire won by 36 runs

Racecourse Ground, Hereford on 16–17 July 1919
Result: Match drawn

County Ground, New Road, Worcester on 18–19 July 1919
Result: Australian Imperial Forces won by an innings and 203 runs

By now it was peak cricket season and the AIF XI's itinerary was appropriately hectic. Three two-day matches in six days saw the team race around the Midlands playing matches in Derby, Hereford and Worcester.

The Derbyshire side assembled to meet the AIF at the County Ground was on paper one of the weakest of the tour. They were largely made up of pre-war players, without a past or future Test player in the side, and they had not put up much of a show in the Championship matches they had played that season, particularly with the bat. Although restricted to 181 in their first innings on a true pitch, the confusion they caused the Australian bowlers is evidenced by six AIF players having a bowl.

In contrast, Derbyshire only called on the services of Horsley (6-55) and Morton (4-66) to bowl the Australians out for just 125, Trenerry's 69 the solitary bright spot.

In the second innings the Australians returned to type; only Gregory (6-65) and Collins (4-39) were needed to bowl the home side out for 112, leaving the AIF 169 runs required for the victory. Horsley took another six wickets, Morton again his chief assistant with three, Murray's half-century alone offering any resistance as the visitors fell 36 runs short of victory to suffer their second defeat, and first – and only – to a county side, of the tour.

Bill Trenerry

Bill Trenerry was one of the least decorated cricketers in the AIF XI. His entire first-class career, with the exception of three matches for New South Wales following the war, was on this tour. Unknown to the cricketing public outside Sydney, he must have shown some promise in grade cricket before the war, being one of Jack Davis' earliest suggested players when the tour was first mooted back in 1917, by which time Trenerry's war service had distinguished him in Australia.

Trenerry enlisted as soon as he could; on his reckoning he was the 323rd member of the AIF. He was first sent to Gallipoli, where he received his first war injuries when the 'Leach Catapult' – more like a slingshot/crossbow – that he was using to launch bombs at the Turkish lines malfunctioned:

> At about 2200 I went into support trench to relieve the sentry then on duty. My first knowledge of the bomb was the burning of the fuse near my feet. I immediately made for safety in one of the tunnels and as I entered the tunnel heard an explosion and felt myself hit in the arm. I then returned

> to enquire if the sentry had been hit. He answered 'No'. I proceeded at once to have my wound dressed. My first knowledge of Private Barrett having been hit was on meeting him at the dressing station.[30]

Following the evacuation from Gallipoli, Trenerry was sent to France. At the battle of Poziers he was wounded once again, struck by shrapnel on the nose and in the helmet. More tragically, his brother Harrie was killed in the battle, pressing a forward attack on the German trenches. His brief recovery mostly consisted of taking a Lewis machine gun course before being shipped off to Flanders. He would put that training to good use. His actions on Tuesday, 14 November 1916 during the Battle of the Ancre, the last movement in the Battle of the Somme, saw Trenerry awarded the Military Cross.

Attacks of 25th, 26th and 5th Battalions all failed. Confusion at the front reigned after communications were

---

30 Quote taken from Peter McGuinness, *Boldly And Faithfully: The Official History of the 19th Australian Infantry Battalion (The South Sydney Regiment) Australian Imperial Force*, (1/19 RNSWR Association incorporating 2/19 Australian Infantry Battalion, 2011), p. 60.

cut, delaying continued attacks and allowing the Germans to retake their positions. His commendation reads:

> In the attack on the gird trenches near Flers on the 14th November 1916, this Officer was in command of the Lewis Machine Guns and displayed great gallantry and coolness under fire. After the position had been captured and the troops on the right of the 19th Battalion had retired, he was given command of the right flank. During the night of 14/15th November he was attacked by enemy's bombing parties and each time repelled them. He showed an excellent example to his men and was responsible for the right flank being held securely, until relieved the following day.

His twin, Les, also won the Military Cross fighting in France and survived the war. In later life William told the story that Les would have probably joined him on the AIF XI tour. However, when the time for the selection trials came around, Les was struck down with Spanish flu, which ultimately claimed his life.

Although not one of the stars of the AIF XI, William Trenerry was a dependable batsman. He played in 24 of the 27 matches, finishing with a respectable first-class batting average of 28.26 that included ten half-centuries and a highest score of 82 against Lancashire, and 118 in the non-first-class match against West of Scotland. He was also an occasional change bowler, a position which did not allow him any great feats during the main part of the tour, but did land him a five-fer against Mitcham in the final match.

HK Foster's XI

The next match was at the Racecourse Ground, Hereford, against HK Foster's XI, one of just six first-class matches the ground would host in its existence. The scratch side included veterans Willie Quaife, who toured Australia with Archie MacLaren's side in 1901/02, and Frank Phillips who met Jack Blackham's 1893 Australians while a student at Oxford. There were also a number of Worcestershire players, including Maurice Jewell, who had just returned to the county after spending the war playing cricket in Sussex and would captain Worcestershire for five seasons in the 1920s. His brother Arthur, who had recently moved to England from South

Africa (both being in the very rare club of Chilean-born first-class cricketers), also played. And of course, Henry Knollys Foster himself.

HK's father Henry had been the housemaster at Malvern College since the 1870s and was one of seven brothers who all played for Worcestershire – his sister Cicely played for England – making the family a local cricketing institution. Henry made his debut for the county at the tender age of just 14. He captained Worcestershire for 11 seasons from their first match in the Championship in 1899 and scored over 1,000 runs in a season eight times. Despite never playing for England he captained the Gentlemen of England on several occasions, and was an English racquets champion 15 times.

This was definitely one of the least serious matches on the tour. HK declared the first innings at 224/9, allowing the Australians some time to bat on the first day and giving those only able to attend day one a chance to see some Australian batting. And bat they did. At stumps Trenerry and Oldfield were set with the score 69/0. Trenerry did not last long into day two, but a Johnny Taylor century helped the visitors to a first-innings score of 405, while the local bowlers did their part, 'extras' the second highest scorer on 62! Needing 180 to make the AIF bat again, and nowhere near enough time left in the day, Foster's men came out swinging in their second innings, leaving them well in arrears on 131/4 when time forced the conclusion.

Johnny Taylor

Johnny Taylor was another of the players mentioned from the very start of the AIF XI discussion. He was an impressive youngster for Gordon Cricket Club and Newington College, where he also starred at rugby union, athletics and rifle shooting. He made his first-class debut in the 1913/14 season for New South Wales while still a schoolboy before he had even played grade cricket, scoring an impressive 83 on debut playing alongside his hero Victor Trumper. Taylor's war service was largely uneventful. After arriving in England in April 1917, he was immediately seconded to the cricket team for the charity matches that summer, meaning he missed the Battle of Passchendaele. He spent a little time on the Western Front in the winter of 1917/18, until a knee complaint took him back to England in time for the 1918 charity cricket matches, before again returning to France for the winter.

Taylor was a regular contributor with the bat on the tour, scoring three centuries, including a high score of 146 against Essex at Southend-on-Sea. On the South African leg of the tour he caught a nasty bout of dysentery, the impact of which would stay with him for the next 12 years. Despite this disability Taylor became a regular in the Test side following the war, playing in 20 Tests in Australia's next five series. He also played two rugby union Tests for Australia in 1922. Although somewhat forgotten amongst Australia's pantheon of leading batsmen with a Test average of 35.6, Oldfield believed without the dysentery he would have been 'spoken of in the same terms as Trumper', while he was the boyhood hero – and batting model – for none other than Don Bradman.

Worcestershire

The final match of the busy week took place at the County Ground, Worcester, versus Worcestershire against many of those players they had faced against HK Foster's XI. Worcestershire CCC had decided to sit out the 1919 County Championship. With an end-of-war surplus balance of £500, the club's grandees were so pessimistic about the prospect of post-war first-class cricket that it was decided to employ just two professionals and arrange a handful of friendly fixtures against county sides and the AIF XI.

The Australians once again had the run of play. Albert Lampard had Worcestershire opener Arthur Jewell out caught and bowled, but other than that wicket it was a Gregory masterclass, 'The Streak' taking seven wickets and catching another two as the home side limped to 120. Trenerry and Oldfield opened steadily for the AIF, taking the score to 103 before both fell in the space of a few balls. Taylor and Murray both fell cheaply with Pellew at the other end and the Australians were 150/4. Then Willis came to the wicket. At the end of day one both were still in, Pellew just having reached his hundred, with the score at 252. The pair continued in the same vein the following morning as both batsmen blasted the Worcestershire bowling. In the end the home side had no answer and Willis finished on 129 not out, with Pellew still beside him on 195 – the highest individual score of the tour – captain Collins cruelly deciding that sending the hosts in and trying to force the result was the better choice than allowing Pellew to reach his double ton. Gregory once again starred with the ball and in the field, taking four wickets and two catches as Worcestershire struggled to 127, giving the AIF XI a commanding innings-and-205-run-victory.

It is also worth noting the absence of Frank Chester from the Worcestershire XI. From 1912-14, while still a teenager, Chester had played as a left-handed middle-order batsman and slow left-arm bowler for Worcestershire. He became the youngest player to score a county century when, as a 17-year-old, he had made 108 against Somerset in 1913. Chester received personal congratulations from cricket's Grand Old Man, WG Grace, for a further century he made at Lord's and looked set for great things.

During the war, Chester served in the Royal Field Artillery in a battery commanded by Major Allsopp, captain of the county's second XI. In July, disaster struck the promising cricketer in the form of a piece of shrapnel, which entered his right arm when an ammunition dump he was guarding came under enemy aerial attack. After several failed attempts to remove the invasive metal, the arm grew gangrenous and had to be amputated. His meteoric cricket rise had come to a painful and debilitating end.

Determined not to drift away from the game and on the advice of Pelham Warner, Chester trained as an umpire, joining the first-class list in 1922. Fearlessly fair, he gave out both captains, Johnny Douglas and John Daniell, in his first match and rose to become the most respected umpire in the land during the inter-war period. He even earned the plaudits of Don Bradman, who rated him as the best umpire he had played under. Chester was to turn disaster into triumph, raising umpiring to a higher level than had ever been known in the history of cricket.

Chapter 18

Warwickshire, Notts, Surrey and Sussex

Warwickshire

Edgbaston, Birmingham on 21–22 July 1919
Result: Australian Imperial Forces won by an innings and 38 runs

Next it was to Edgbaston for a two-day match against Warwickshire. The Warwickshire XI was a combination of the old and new, ranging from the now 47-year-old former Test batsman Willie Quaife, to 1918 schoolboy *Wisden* Cricketer of the Year Gerard Rotherham. Tiger Smith, who had played 11 Tests before the war, helped bolster the side. More familiar to the Australians was the Reverend E.F. 'Mick' Waddy. Waddy came from Sydney and had been a member of the New South Wales XI before the war. He courted controversy in 1906 when he backed the NSWCA in a dispute with the players over the control of New South Wales cricket. Right before the outbreak of war he had organised and managed an NSW tour of Ceylon that included Collins, Kelleway and Docker, as well as Eric Barbour, Syd Gregory, Warren Bardsley, Victor Trumper, Charlie Macartney, Ashley Minnett, Harry Hordern and Claude Tozer. That he had such ties to Australian cricket management, and so many of the players who either were members or potential members of the AIF XI, makes it surprising his name was never among those touted as organisers for the tour. This is quite possibly because it would have conflicted with his teaching duties at Rugby School.

The Reverend did his adopted home side proud, more than doubling any of his team-mates' scores with 73 runs out of a first-innings team total of 215. Collins was the chief destroyer with the ball, taking 5-73, and the bat, his 110 ably supported by 52 from Willis and 45 not out from Lampard. The Australians scored 321 in their first innings, leaving 117 needed from Warwickshire to force the Australians to bat again. Only Winning and Stirling were needed as bowlers as they knocked the home side over for just 68 runs in a touch over 40 overs, JH Parsons'

13 the lone double figures in the batting column. The AIF XI were victorious by an innings and 38 runs.

Charles Winning was one of the players who went to the selection trials in April 1919, but did not make the cut. He would have to wait until Kelleway returned home before claiming his permanent spot in the side. His AIF XI appearances were the only first-class matches of his cricketing career. He had been a promising prospect prior to the war, playing for NSW colts in 1914. He was a good all-round athlete, also playing rugby union for Paddington, and A grade baseball. His very first ball in first-class cricket resulted in Hearne being caught in the slips. Although he ended the tour with the second-lowest batting average, his role in the tail was to stay in, like he did in the first match against Sussex. This resulted in him being not out 11 times from 24 innings, more than any other player in the team.

Nottinghamshire

Trent Bridge, Nottingham on 24–26 July 1919
Result: Match drawn

The next side to meet the AIF XI were Nottinghamshire at Trent Bridge. In the Nottinghamshire side were John and George Gunn, Joe Hardstaff, who toured Australia in 1907/08, Len Richmond, one of the players tried out during the 1921 Ashes, a young Fred Barratt, at the start of a long career for Notts that culminated in selection for the 1929 and 1929/30 Ashes squads, Notts legends Garnett Lee, Tom Oates and Wilf Payton and one of the *Wisden* Cricketers of the Year in 1918, John Firth, who eschewed a cricket career to become chaplain at Winchester College.

Collins (71) and Taylor (60) anchored the AIF innings, before Willis (130) and Oldfield (65) brought the Australian innings home with a 169-run partnership bringing their first-innings total to 371. The Nottinghamshire bowling was all at sea, demonstrated by their use of nine bowlers during the innings.

Opener George Gunn did his best to chase the total, scoring 131, ably assisted by Hardstaff (82) and Payton (50) to hand Nottinghamshire a narrow 20-run lead at the halfway point. That the Australians used six bowlers to complete their innings suggests it was the pitch, more than the batting, confusing the bowlers. The big scores are possibly also attributable to the three-day length of the match, the extra day giving the batting sides space to breathe during their innings. This left them short of playing time, although you would not know that from the Australians' play on the third day, scoring nearly 100 before declaring on 237/5 to set 218 for victory. Notts managed 62 runs for the loss of just one wicket from the remaining 25 overs of play, an exciting match ending in a draw.

Surrey

The Oval, Kennington on 31st July, 1st, 2nd August 1919
Result: Match drawn

There was another reunion at the next match at The Oval against Surrey. Nip Pellew's former schoolmaster Jack Crawford took the field for the home side. Crawford played cricket across the empire, playing first-class cricket for South Australia, Surrey, and Otago in New Zealand. He played Tests for England in 1906 and 1908 and toured with several 'Unofficial' Australian sides. He moved to Australia in 1909 following a dispute with the Surrey committee surrounding selection and was living in New Zealand by the time he enlisted.

This was another three-day match against a strong Surrey side which again boasted five Test players in Jack

Hobbs, Donald Knight, Bill Hitch and Bert Strudwick, along with Crawford. Even the non-Test players were genuine first-class performers: Miles Howell, Tom Rushby, Henry Harrison, Cyril Wilkinson and Frank Naumann all ended their careers with over 50 first-class appearances.

Totally absent were the players whose sole contribution to cricket records were the 1919 season like we see in most matches on the tour.

Once again it was Collins (95), supported by Trenerry (78), Willis (58), and Lampard (58), who led the AIF XI to a strong first-innings total of 436. Rushby shone for the county with six wickets. After a shaky start Wilkinson (103) and Crawford (144) steadied the Surrey innings, moving the score from 83/6 to 229/7, the heart of Surrey's 322-run response.

The third day began with the AIF at 8/1, 122 runs in the lead, with a day's play remaining. Although they set about the task with a bit more purpose than the previous match, in soaking up 69 overs to put on 260 runs, they put the result of the match beyond doubt. In the remaining 33 overs of the day Surrey, led by Hobbs, held on to lose just the one wicket, but still needing over 200 runs for the victory.

Despite the lack of result, the exciting cricket had drawn a crowd of over 20,000 for the three days, rivalling those crowds seen at Test matches before the war.

However, one of those amongst the crowd was not pleased with what he saw as 'over-cautious' tactics by the Australians. The following is from the *Yorkshire Evening Post*:

> The Australians were barracked. The crowd, when once their patience had been exhausted, hooted, hissed, applauded ironically, became restless, fidgeted uneasily in their seats, and then lapsed into slumber or preserved stolid silence.
>
> Then one gentleman in black, with a black bowler hat, and a black look on his face woke suddenly from a deep sleep. He glanced up at the telegraph board and found that only a score of runs had been added during that time to the Colonials' total.
>
> This was too much for him. He shook himself up, bade goodbye to his friends, who were ignorant of his intentions, and strode

> solemnly into the arena. Was he a madman? Did he understand cricket etiquette? Did he know that he was committing an unpardonable sin?
>
> Still he kept his way. He walked up to CB Willis, the Australian batsman, and implored him to get on with the business or get out.
>
> With a few calm words the Surrey captain soothed the angry spectator, who returned to the ring.
>
> However, before reaching his seat, he was so proud at having been the mouthpiece of the multitude that he astonished the crowd with a gymnastic exhibition, and a feeble imitation of Hitch bowling at his fastest.

The correspondent added, 'this proved the only exciting episode of the afternoon'. Not all of the Englishmen agreed with him, one correspondent in the press box saying, 'I have no use for the beery gas workers who invade the pitch. These vulgar persons don't understand the game.'

Sussex

County Ground, Hove on 4th, 5th August 1919
Result: Australian Imperial Forces won by an innings and 54 runs

Following the close contest against Surrey it was off to the County Ground at Hove for a second match against Sussex. Notable inclusions in the side from the first match were future Sussex captain and England bowler Vallance Jupp, past legend and Test cricketer Albert Relf joining his brother Bob, and English football international Stanley Harris. Again, the bowling combination of Gregory and Collins was too much for the home side, the pair sharing all the wickets and most of the overs as Sussex struggled to 120. Willis opened the batting and held his head as his team fell around him, finally being run out on 127, the single major contributor to the Australian score of 300. Collins was once again fierce in the second Sussex innings, taking six wickets. Wilson's 38 was the only significant contribution to the Sussex score of 126, handing the Australians a massive innings-and-54-run victory.

Major CT Docker

Prior to the war Cyril Talbot Docker was a banker 'without much time for the game', which explains why he had just the sole first-class season in 1909/10. A friend of Eric Barbour, he played for Burwood in Sydney grade cricket and in 1914 was selected for Rev. EF Waddy's tour of Ceylon, along with several other future members of the AIF XI. Docker joined in the rush of 1915 and served in Egypt and France. He was mentioned in dispatches for leading a group over the top at Poziers and capturing a German trench, in which he was wounded and consequently treated for 'shell shock'.

Docker played in several of the 1917 matches, including the charity match at Lord's. However, complications from his injuries gave him a sensitivity to light and he served the remainder of the war behind a desk. His initial involvement in the AIF XI was in an organisational capacity, before being selected for the side. The tour would be the end of his first-class career. Following the war he continued his career in banking, working for the English, Scottish and Australian Bank Ltd for 40 years, rising to chief inspector, the second highest position in the bank in Australia.

Chapter 19

Second Scotland Trip

Greenock

Glenpark, Greenock, 15 August 1919
Result: Australian Imperial Forces won by 101 runs

The original schedule had the team set to travel to Ireland following the Northamptonshire match. It is perhaps indicative of the state of Irish cricket that the reason for the cancellation was the absence of the intended host, rather than any logistical difficulties in getting a match or three together on the Emerald Isle.

Sir Stanley Cochrane was the heir to a ginger ale empire; his father, Henry, was one of the inventors of the beverage. Upon inheritance in 1904 Stanley went about spending his vast fortune on, among other interests, growing cricket in Ireland. This included bringing the 1905 Australians over to play a single match against

Dublin University Past and Present for the giant match fee of £300, contributing to one of the most financially successful tours for Australian players until the 1980s.

The cricketing extravagance continued with the creation of the Woodbrook Cricket Club on the grounds of his estate, and the construction of a railway station to service the crowds he anticipated drawing to his ground. The ground peaked in 1912 with a visit from the South Africans to play against Woodbrook in a game with dubious first-class credentials. An attempt to get one of the Test matches of the Triangular Tournament was rebuffed, and Stanley closed the ground in protest and turned his attention to golf.

The visit from the 1919 Australians seems to have been an attempt to rejuvenate cricketing interest in Ireland. However, urgent business in America called him away, leading to the tour being cancelled. Given what was to come in the following years where sporting matches would become targets for terror from both sides of the war of independence, one wonders if someone had a word in Sir Stanley's ear that such a display of the empire's military may not be as popular in Dublin as he was hoping. Regardless of the reasons, cricket was mostly lost in what would become the

Republic of Ireland from then, virtually banned until the 1970s.[31]

Fortunately for the AIF XI, another beverage tycoon, Scottish whisky distiller Peter Dawson, invited the team north for a 'motor tour' of Scotland, taking in sights such as Loch Ness and travelling as far north as Inverness. Garden parties with the social elite, tours of factories with business magnates – including a trip to see some newly manufactured submarines – and a visit to Blair Atholl Castle to be entertained by the duke, were all part of the itinerary. After such a gruelling schedule of cricket, where even a day that did not involve at least a train trip was a rarity, this was sweet relief for the men who, let us not forget, had just recently fought in a war.

Of course, there was *some* cricket. The first contest was a single-innings, one-day match against Greenock, the home side of the Scottish captain John Kerr, who played against the Australians on their first trip to

---

31 Cricket was never banned in Ireland per se, but playing cricket would get an athlete banned from the Gaelic Athletic Association, the governing body for most other sports played in the Republic of Ireland. This had the effect that no decent Irish athlete would risk a ban in all sports just to play a cricket match.

Scotland earlier in the tour. A large crowd greeted the Australians, likely ready for the inevitable drubbing that was coming the home side's way. Murray scored 121, but the rest of the side struggled against Kerr's bowling, his 5-62 stunting any start an Australian made. Chasing 284, Kerr and his opening partner JB Walker put on an impressive opening stand before Walker fell for 48. Kerr valiantly held on for a century of his own before falling to Pellew, but just one other player could breach double figures as Collins ripped through the lower-quality Scottish batsmen, taking eight wickets at the meagre cost of 39 runs.

North of Scotland

Northern Meeting Park, Inverness, 16 August 1919
Result: Match drawn

The AIF XI next travelled to Inverness to meet a North of Scotland XV. The Australians batted first; the Scots' bowling and fielding 'proved quite satisfactory' in restricting the AIF to 196. However, the difference in the two sides was brought into stark relief when the home side batted. Collins and Winning both took six wickets apiece for under 20 runs, while the batting side featured three top scores of 6 and included six ducks in a total of 36. With still over an hour of light left, the AIF went in to provide some entertainment to the crowd that now numbered in their thousands. Whether they found their form, or had just been playing carefully in the first innings, now it was no holds barred. It took just 35 minutes to pass the 100-run mark. Sixes were hit by Docker, Murray and Bull, who scored a half-century. Ernie Cameron, who had opened the batting, was still in on 50 when stumps were called, the Australians scoring 178 runs in just over an hour of cricket.

Chapter 20

Essex

Southchurch Park, Southend-on-Sea on 21–23 August 1919
Result: Australian Imperial Forces won by 309 runs

The AIF's first match back in England after their Scottish tour was against Essex at Southend-on-Sea. Despite the distance between this and their last match at Inverness being the greatest of the tour, they had five days to make the journey – their longest break of the season – and were well rested on arrival.

Playing for the home side once again was Johnny Douglas. In glorious weather in front of a large crowd the English star made short work of the AIF XI batting line-up, taking 7-50 to have the Australians bundled out for 130, Murray's 30 the best effort. In reply Gregory and Collins took four wickets each, restricting Essex to

150. and presented a tight second-innings contest to the crowd. The visitors were having none of it. Taylor put on a batting masterclass for his 146 runs, ably supported by Collins (43), Pellew (57), Willis (41) and Murray (82), as the AIF rocketed to 440/8 before declaring to give the bowlers a chance to take all ten Essex wickets and get a result. Douglas once again led the bowling attack, but was expensive, leaking 168 runs for his four wickets. In the final innings Gregory again led the bowling, his 5-34 the lynchpin in having Essex all out for 117, handing the Australians victory by 309 runs.

The big story of the week was not the AIF XI, but the future of cricket in England for both the County Championship and Test matches. As noted, the Championship had moved to two-day matches in 1919. The intention was to allow for more spectators to attend as more matches would be on Saturday and games on weekdays would end later, while also reducing the workload on the players, and the expense on the county.

However, by now it was clear to all the scheme was a failure. Rather than reducing the workload on the players, it made it worse, as players were now finding themselves going straight from the ground to catch the train home rather than the traditional bath and dinner they enjoyed in previous years.

Rather than feeling refreshed by playing fewer days of cricket, the longer playing hours of the two-day system left players feeling 'absolutely stale'. With the draw card of the AIF XI, as well as the uncertainty surrounding how the game would recover after the war anyway, it is hard to determine if the expected financial benefits were realised – having to pay one day's fewer wages to players and saving on one night's accommodation did not have the impact the two-day supporters expected. Likewise on the crowd front. Crowds were good in 1919, but how much of this was to do with longer hours, and how much was the excitement built by the AIF XI, or just the return to cricket in general, is unquantifiable. However, it was noted two-day matches often ended in a draw, and good cricket was often abandoned in favour of batting out the clock. For the true cricket aficionado, the benefit of the game running a few hours longer into the evening would not have made up for the lack of 'brighter cricket'. As such, the scheme was abandoned and the Championship would return to three-day matches from 1920.

Also announced was MCC rejecting the Australian offer to tour in 1920. This is quite interesting. It was clear by now Australian teams would once again 'draw' like they did in the pre-war days. A full Australian tour would be a financial benefit for every county in the land. However, quite probably because of the strength of the AIF XI, those in control of English cricket deemed it too soon for a full Ashes tour, thinking 'there is enough to do in getting back to the old system of county cricket as played before the war'. This is a clear indication the financial pressures on the counties had been eased by the AIF XI tour. No longer was the very existence of the clubs in question, and focus could be returned to finding the next generation of young cricketers to take on the Australians. This is supported by Lord Harris' comments as conveyed to the counties in a cable from FE Lacey:[32]

> Lord Harris is personally very doubtful whether English fast bowling will by the date suggested warrant a team going to Australia

---

32 Lacey initially cabled the counties to let them know the ABC had sent a telegram suggesting Australia send a team in 1920, and England return in 1920/21. A few hours later he sent the same telegram, but with Harris' comments added, giving them the weight of the final word.

> next year with much hope of success; but he has no opportunity of consulting leading Cricketers at the moment.

As we have seen through this tour, many counties had chosen pre-war players well past their prime rather than risk promising youngsters. The impetus to 'rebuild cricket' in general had been so strong that rebuilding future playing stocks had taken a back seat in the 1919 season.

The team the English did finally send out to Australia for the first post-war Ashes series in 1920/21 was far from second-rate: Johnny Douglas, Jack Hearne, Wilfred Rhodes, Patsy Hendren, Jack Hobbs and Harry Makepeace reads like a team of champions. However, they were absolutely embarrassed in the Test series, suffering the first ever 5-0 whitewash. The confusion continued to the next series in 1921, when seemingly everyone in England who fancied themselves a cricketer got a run in a Test match. It is of course not provable, but one wonders whether the difference came down to the opportunity the Australians had to establish themselves *as a team* as the AIF XI.

Chapter 21

Festival Cricket

BY THE early 20th century the concept of a 'cricket week' or 'festival cricket' had become common at many locations across England, particularly holiday resorts. Crowds would flock to grounds such as St Lawrence in Canterbury, North Marine Road in Scarborough, the Central Recreation Ground in Hastings, Clifton College in Bristol and the College in Cheltenham to see two well-matched sides made up of some of the greatest cricketers available do battle. This would be accompanied by fêtes, parades and markets in the town by day, and concerts, dinners and balls by night. The atmosphere at the ground was a lively affair, often hosting bands and 'ladies' days'.

While some, such as Canterbury Week at Kent, were in the peak of the cricketing season in early August, the real excitement came after the County Championship had concluded, allowing for representative matches such as South v North, Gentlemen v Players, or scratch sides like we have already seen such as the LG Robinson and HK Foster XIs. In years when international sides visited these were a common way to end the tour. Australian teams had a venerable tradition of being major draws at such festivals. The 1878 touring side had appeared at Clifton College, Scarborough, Hove and Hastings. In more recent years, all Australian teams of the early 20th century had played in the Scarborough and Hastings Festivals, with most also turning out at grounds such as Cheltenham and Canterbury.

In the space of 14 days at the end of August and start of September, the AIF played matches at three of the great festivals: the Clifton Festival, where they met Gloucestershire; the Cricket Festival at Hastings, against a combined South of England XI; and the Scarborough Festival, where they faced CI Thornton's XI – as close as the Australians would get to playing 'England'. However, as this was the great promotional juggernaut that was the AIF XI, they also had a match against Somerset CCC at Taunton, and a second match against South of England at Portsmouth.

When the tour itinerary was first drawn up there must have been hope that the inclusion of matches at Canterbury, Clifton College, Hastings, and Scarborough would help publicise the return of these beloved festivals. A successful tour that *could* and maybe *should* have included a Test match had the crowds at fever pitch by the time the matches against the South and CI Thornton's XI came around.

Kent

St Lawrence Ground, Canterbury on 7–9 August 1919
Result: Match drawn

When war was declared in August 1914 the Canterbury Week closed down, the first time in history that external events had spoiled the fun. The cricket, with its concomitant theatricals and balls, was declared off limits. The country had no place for festivals in the subsequent four years.

The revival of the Canterbury Festival, which, with a tradition stretching back to 1842, was the oldest festival in cricket, was overshadowed by the unveiling of the memorial to the most prominent English cricketer to have given his life in the recent war – Colin Blythe.

The Times reported on 8 August 1919 on how the memories of war intermingled with the gaiety of the events surrounding the playing of cricket.

FIELDERS DISTURBED BY FLAPPERS

Ladies Day in Canterbury Week came this year in glorious sunshine, and during the play the spectators saw a host of those incidents, which, with their element of surprise, contribute to cricket half its fascination, and make a first-class match an engrossing spectacle, even for those who have never played.

Before the confetti and general litter left by the carnival had been swept from the streets, a long processional of motor cars was travelling towards the St Lawrence Ground, and behind the bevelled windows one caught sight now and then of a lorgnette or saw the flutter of coloured silk or muslin or cotton, and there were hundreds of people walking too. Many of them were in time to see the cadre of the 7th Buffs,

> home from the occupied territories, march through the city to the Cathedral, where in the Warriors' Chapel its colours were deposited. At the cricket ground there were more motor cars than ever, and the crowd was the biggest this week.

The reporter also noted 'flappers' joyfully collecting the autographs of Australian players as the Kent opening batsmen were nearly at the wicket. One's social class was evident by the type of victuals one brought for the lunch interval: 'Those who come in motor cars bring hampers well stocked with meats and pies and wines, and these they devour on the roof of the car or in one of the many reserved marquees.'

A second type arrived 'with pockets strained by the presence of bottles and sandwiches' while others 'rely on the arrangements made by the club to which they belong'.

After luncheon, the writer noted the changing styles of the ladies parading on the outfield, 'At one time there would have been the skirts of stately ladies trailing upon the turf, but the skirts of today do not trail, and whether they cover age or youth they are uniformly short and brilliant and diaphanous'. Chatter would be heard about the cricket and 'a little scandal'.

Of the players taking to the field on 7 August 1919, the first day of the Kent v AIF match at the St Lawrence Ground in Canterbury, four were survivors of the previous time an Australian XI had graced the festival in 1912.

Frank Woolley was one of the greatest all-rounders the game has ever seen. By 1919 he had already taken the 100 wicket/1,000 run double on three occasions – in 1910, 1912 and 1914 – a feat he would accomplish eight times. 1919 was the only season out of his 29 he would not score 1,000 first-class runs for Kent; more a statement on the lack of matches than Woolley's ability, for once his first-class matches for South, Players, LG Robinson's XI, and The Rest are included he took the double again. The stats and records go on and are far too many. Suffice to say, here was one of the games GOATs, at the peak of his abilities.

On the other hand, Wally Hardinge's stats do not serve him any justice. It is easy to look past the 1,000 runs in a season 18 times, or his 55 first division football matches, and see solitary England caps in football and cricket. Definitely a great all-round athlete who couldn't quite break the top tier. This ignores his employer's refusal to grant leave in 1928/29, or the missed cricket tours due to professional football obligations. Here was another great batsman, possibly overlooked, especially by Australian audiences.

Veteran all-rounder Edward 'Punter' Humphreys was coming to the end of two decades of service to the county. Bill Fairservice had lived up to his moniker and would be rewarded with a benefit season of £1,196 – a remuneration that would have come earlier but for the hiatus of war.

The match itself was drawn. Diminutive Kent leg-spinner AP 'Tich' Freeman, who had played but a handful of matches in 1914 before war interrupted his development, tore the heart out of the AIF first innings, taking the wickets of Trennery, Taylor and Pellew. They would go into a career account which would end with a tally of 3,776 first-class dismissals, second on the all-time list behind only Wilfred Rhodes. That the AIF XI would be meeting the two most prolific first-class bowlers in history on this tour shows that, in retrospect, the concern over the quality of the cricket was way off the mark – especially for the English.

Jack Gregory passed 100 wickets for the season when dismissing Tich in the hosts' first innings. Herbie

Collins' declaration left Kent three hours to score the 317 runs needed for victory. Despite a forcing 76 from Woolley, both sides emerged with a creditable draw, and, perhaps more significantly, one part of a fine Kent cricketing tradition was firmly re-established.

However, the customary dances normally associated with the festival match were absent in 1919. With nearly a million men who had served in the British and Commonwealth forces confirmed dead, or still on the agonising missing lists, such frivolity was considered a step too far. However, the conclusion of the festival saw the Old Stagers put on a performance of *Worzel Flummery* at the local theatre, followed by a 'Brighter Cricket' epilogue, a tradition that would extend through the next world war and beyond.

Clifton Week
Gloucestershire

Clifton College Close Ground, Clifton on 27–28 August 1919
Result: Match drawn

Where Kent led, Gloucestershire followed. Both the Cheltenham College and Clifton College grounds had played host to previous iterations of Australian tourists. However, there had been a lacuna of 15 years since Gloucestershire had used the latter for first-class fixtures. The 1919 Clifton Cricket Week revival festival would feature the hosts firstly against Essex and then the Australians. 'This Clifton Week completes the Gloucestershire programme for 1919' announced the *Western Daily Press*. The *Gloucestershire Echo* carried advertisements of cars running from Gloucester and Cheltenham to the cricket on a daily basis, 'Fare 25/- Return' – about equivalent to a week's wages.

It was fitting that first-class cricket – and an AIF team in particular – should return to Clifton College immediately following the years in which so many young men had heeded the call to 'Play Up! Play the Game!' CEW Bean, the official historian for the AIF, founder of the Australian War Memorial, and arguably the inventor of the Anzac myth, was an old boy, as were Field Marshal Haig and General Birdwood. As was the case with the Canterbury match, the shadow of war cast over the festival spirit, as the Australian players and officials observed a silent toast during a dinner at the college. Henry Newbolt's invocation to Britain's elite youth, *Vitai Lampada*, had been set in the 'Close', the Clifton College Close Ground. Although the 'sodden red' desert sand in the poem refers to the Battle of Abu Klea in Sudan in 1885, it became somewhat of a secular prayer during the First World War, especially among grammar school-educated soldier-athletes, which so many cricketers were.

Vitai Lampada

('They Pass On The Torch of Life')

There's a breathless hush in the Close
to-night –
Ten to make and the match to win –
A bumping pitch and a blinding light,
An hour to play and the last man in.
And it's not for the sake of a
ribboned coat,
Or the selfish hope of a season's fame,
But his Captain's hand on his
shoulder smote –
'Play up! play up! and play the game!'

The sand of the desert is sodden red, –
Red with the wreck of a square
that broke; –
The Gatling's jammed and the

Colonel dead,
And the regiment blind with
dust and smoke.
The river of death has brimmed his banks,
And England's far, and Honour a name,
But the voice of a schoolboy
rallies the ranks:
'Play up! play up! and play the game!'

This is the word that year by year,
While in her place the School is set,
Every one of her sons must hear,
And none that hears it dare forget.
This they all with a joyful mind
Bear through life like a torch in flame,
And falling fling to the host behind –
'Play up! play up! and play the game!'

The efforts undertaken to revive the festival were overshadowed by inclement weather. The *South Bristol Free Press* later bemoaned, 'The receipts for the Clifton Cricket Week amounted to £17. If the weather had been fine, £1,000 was estimated as the takings.' Gloucestershire had packed their side with holidaying amateurs, just Alf

Dipper, Charlie Parker and Harry Smith appearing as professionals. Dipper, known affectionately as 'Old Dip', had been one of the first professional county cricketers to heed his country's call in August 1914. Indeed, so keen was he to rush to the colours that he left his county in the middle of a match against Surrey, leaving them to take the field with ten men. He was welcomed back into the fold in 1919 and would be another player whose one and only brush with Test cricket would come against the 1921 Australian tourists, during which he would far from disgrace himself with scores of 40 and 11.

The first day belonged to Gloucestershire, who amassed 281 all out. 'Quite the feature of the match', opined *Wisden*, 'was the reappearance of CL Townsend.' One of a famous Gloucestershire cricketing dynasty that was eclipsed only by the Graces, Townsend first appeared for the county while a schoolboy at Clifton College and was named one of *Wisden*'s Five Cricketers of the Year in 1899, the year he also played his only two Test matches. Townsend had faded somewhat from the game during the 1900s, making just three first-class appearances across the seven pre-war seasons, all in festival matches. It was remarkable, given his long absence from big cricket, that Townsend top-scored in

Gloucestershire's innings with 63, batting finely, driving with great power. In the 90 minutes remaining of the day Parker and Dipper ripped through the Australian opening order to have them 104/6 overnight, Gregory's 50 alone providing some resistance.

Rain prevented any play before 4pm on the second day of a match only allotted two days in the first place. The AIF, having followed on 134 runs behind the hosts, limped to 64/6 in their second innings in 39 overs. Charlie Parker, whose outspoken character ensured that he too would remain a one-Test 1921 wonder, claimed ten Australian wickets for 91 in the match.

Somerset

County Ground, Taunton on 29–30 August 1919
Result: Australian Imperial Forces won by 95 runs

Before continuing on the festival circuit, the AIF XI had one final game against a county side, meeting Somerset at the County Ground in Taunton. There was little actual play in the rain-affected two-day match, but this did not prevent a result. Somerset legends Ernie Robson (6-45) and Jack White (4-35) had the Australians bundled out for 85 when rain ended play on day one. Collins (4-38) and Winning (6-30) returned the favour to hand a surprising 15-run lead to the AIF XI. Collins, Gregory and Willis all batted with intent and the visitors declared at 144, leaving 160 the victory target with a few hours left in the day and clouds looming overhead. However, Collins made the game his own, taking eight Somerset wickets to have the home side out for just 64 runs.

As was customary on a cricket tour, one of the big attractions was a dinner with the players hosted by the local club. This gave local dignitaries a chance to show their hospitality and give their thanks to the soldier cricketers. Following the Somerset game there was such a dinner, where the Bishop of Taunton gave a speech that captured the essence of the AIF XI:

> We have learnt much during the last five years – before the war we had learnt a little – of what our Empire meant. We had learnt in those five years what we had to lose for the Empire, but we had also learnt some of these things which we might win through the war, and that some of the things which we believed before the war to be true were really so, that our Empire was a known force.

United as we had been, we had learnt in a wondrous way what it meant to the Empire's strength.

God grant that that strength might never decrease, but that we might remain united in peace as we had been in war. It was almost a byword how splendidly the Empire responded when we were in trouble, and it was splendid the way they came to the call to the old Mother Country, and they went out to fight side by side together and learnt that we were indeed of one blood and one great nation and Empire.

We had a great vision before us of what that Empire might be in the future now that the war had so bound it together. He only wished that as with cricket, so might it be with politics, that our politicians might run as straight and play the game as straight as the cricketers from Australia did and had done and then it would be good for our old Empire both beyond the seas and at home.

Hastings
South of England

Central Recreation Ground, Hastings on 1–3 September 1919
Result: South won by 122 runs

Any remaining summer shadows were lengthening as the AIF made their way to the Sussex resort of Hastings to take on a South of England XI for the first of two matches in the first week of September. The Central Recreation Ground had a less venerable festival tradition than Canterbury and Scarborough but could boast the appearance of WG Grace on no fewer than 40 occasions.

The South XI selected to face the AIF XI included the peerless Frank Woolley, Hampshire run machine Phil Mead, and future England skipper Arthur Gilligan. The near full-strength South of England side was missing 'just a few Surrey men' and included seven Test players. The South handled clever Australian bowling on a tricky wicket to eke out 183 runs from their first innings. In reply, only Willis found form, his 54 keeping the AIF within 21 runs. On day two Phil Mead took the game by the scruff of the neck under leaden Sussex skies. He lit up proceedings, scoring 75 batting in 'his best form' according to *Wisden*. His 87-run partnership with Wally Hardinge, who 'played in an attractive style' for 90, the nucleus around the South innings of 280, left Australia 302 to get, and most of day three to get it.

In contrast the Australians' play drew heavy criticism, scoring at a rate of just 2.11 per over in the final innings as they slumped to a 122-run defeat – just the third loss of the tour. It was fully expected they would display some of the swashbuckling batting that had been electrifying the whole island, but it soon became clear they 'despaired of accomplishing the task, nearly all the batsmen adopting careful unenterprising methods'. It was a disappointment for the crowd, for many of whom a do-or-die approach to the task of chasing a winning total was the stuff of cricket festivals.

South of England

United Services Ground, Portsmouth on 4–5 September 1919
Result: Australian Imperial Forces won by ten wickets

Although not a festival, with all the attendant sideshows, the second match against the South at the seaside resort of Portsmouth attracted a similar holiday crowd, this time with the added excitement of seeing a side that had finally been able to bring down the Australians. The South also lost Woolley and Hardinge, and although some 'attractive batsmen' came in, this was an arguably weaker team, although contemporary commentators felt the two South sides were of equal strength. Day one belonged to Gregory who, once he got the breakthrough wicket of George Brown to have the South at 59/2, shredded the batting, taking six wickets as the home side tumbled for 104.

Gregory was one of those bowlers who went from being 'good' to 'deadly' when he found that extra turn of speed. Unfortunately, his bowling efforts seemed to have taken it out of him as he fell for a duck when opening the Australian innings. The AIF batting depth came to the fore, and while no one stood out, there were enough starts from the batsmen to have them 102 ahead when the South went in to bat for the second time. This time it was the turn of Stirling (three wickets) and Winning's (five wickets) turn. They needed just an hour and 50 minutes to demolish the South for 115 runs and left the AIF 14 needed for the win, and more than a day's play to get them. Pellew and Collins easily broke the hearts of fans of a third day, the game finishing early enough to allow the Australians to catch the early train out.

Scarborough Festival
CI Thornton's XI

North Marine Road, Scarborough on 8–10 September 1919
Result: CI Thornton's XI won by two wickets

And so to Scarborough. The Scarborough festival had its origins in the tastes of the wealthy holidaymakers and spa-seekers who would descend on the Yorkshire resort in the summer months. Cricket matches became a locus for social engagements and parading of ladies' fashions. In 1876 Lord Londesborough, then president of MCC, commissioned cricket evangelist CI 'Buns' Thornton to put together a programme of nine days' worth of cricket across late August and early September. The feature match was Yorkshire versus an MCC XI managed by 'Buns'.

For several years Londesborough funded the hospitality of the Gentlemen amateurs invited to perform at the Scarborough Festival. Following his death in 1900, Thornton took on full responsibility for the festival for the next three decades. Australian touring teams became accustomed to seeing out their first-class programme at the North Marine Road Ground, situated within a couple of hundred yards of the North Sea.

It was significant the Scarborough Festival was very much back on the English cricketing calendar. More than many towns, the Yorkshire coastal resort had endured an excess of Teutonic attention during the preceding five years. Following the late decision to entirely cancel the 1914 festival, Lord Hawke had offered the seaside club, on MCC's behalf, 'our very sincere sympathy at the great disappointment our action must cause you all'. The Yorkshire players concurred with the decision, having 'little heart' for festival frolicking. But much worse was to come for Scarborough. On 16 December German naval attacks on the east coast towns of Scarborough, Whitby and Hartlepool caused several hundred civilian casualties, over 100 of them fatal. One of those who had a lucky escape was Scarborough native and Yorkshire CCC cricketer Benny Wilson. The doughty opening batsman had been enjoying a stimulating morning dip in the North Sea when the vessels attacked.

On 4 September 1917, the North Marine Road Ground itself sustained damage when a German shell fired from a submarine hit the outfield. That the waves of war had now literally lapped on to the nation's coastline caused a further shift in attitudes as to how fitting it was to continue with cricket leagues. Scarborough Cricket

Club withdrew from the Yorkshire Council league structure and by 1916 had run up a debt of £395 as the only matches played on the famous old ground were *ad hoc* ones against local military sides. Although not on the same scale as the Lord's matches put on by Pelham Warner, one such fixture raised £23 for the Scarborough Hospital.

Late 1918 had seen tentative steps to revive the festival, even though the formal Armistice which ended the fighting on the Western Front was still a couple of months away. One of the first matches played between Lord Hawke's Yorkshire XI and Lieutenant Colonel Hawdon's XI was delayed until 3.00pm by a sea fret. On the August bank holiday, a Yorkshire County XI played the host club. To complement the war charity cricket, a ball took place at the Grand Hotel, the first function of its kind since September 1913. Over 150 dancers enjoyed a two-and-a-half-hour programme with the cricketers in attendance, as well as local dignitaries and 'many naval and military officers, whose distinctive uniforms added colour to a bright and animated scene'. The ground was also used that summer by two sides of American soldiers to play a baseball match in aid of the British Sailors' War Orphans Fund. As the highlight of the 1919 festival, some of the Australians had expressed a desire that their efforts in reviving international cricket so soon after the conclusion of the war be recognised in granting the Scarborough fixture Test match status. However, when the Test match idea was abandoned, a match against CI Thornton's XI – an invitational side that was effectively 'England' – was organised.

When the Great War interrupted the gathering, the Scarborough Festival had become renowned for the eminent status of the players who performed there. The XI Thornton raised was the strongest English side to take the field since 1912. With the County Championship concluded, the cream of English cricket was available for selection. CI Thornton's XI included a galaxy of proven Test players, including Jack Hobbs, Johnny Douglas, Reggie Spooner, Wilfred Rhodes, George Hirst and Bill Hitch. Indeed, such was the strength of the team Thornton assembled that the *Yorkshire Post*'s *Old Ebor*, Alfred Pullin, opined: 'The official title of the first match this week was Mr CI Thornton's XI v. the Australian Imperial Force. This, however, is too big a mouthful; so we call it an England Eleven v. the Australians.' Hobbs, Douglas, Spooner, Rhodes, Hirst and Hitch would have been strong contenders for any representative England

XI. Indeed, there have been several occasions in Ashes history in which one or other combination of players were inferior quality to those taking part in the festival season finale.

The match itself was blessed with fine late summer weather. Around 6,000 spectators enjoyed the first and second days' play, an orchestra playing during the lunch and tea intervals adding to the gaiety of the scene. On the third day, some of the Yorkshire crowds whose priority was the social scene rather than the cricket opted for the competing attraction of the St Leger Festival in Doncaster.

The Scarborough wicket was prone to favouring the faster bowlers. Hitch and Gregory took six and seven wickets respectively during each side's first innings. The AIF XI were dismissed for a paltry 81 on the first day but managed to restrict Thornton's XI to a lead of 106. A far better muster second time around realised a total of 296, leaving the Englishmen a target of 191 for victory. Had it not been for the presence of the world's premier batsman, Jack Hobbs, in their side, it is likely the AIF would have ended their first-class campaign with another victory. He made 93 of the successful run chase. Another world-class performer, Wilfred Rhodes, who possibly had the steadiest judgement and most unflappable temperament in cricket, was there at the end to guide Thornton's XI to a two-wicket win. 'The defeat did [the AIF XI] more credit than any of their victories,' read the *Wisden* match report. The fielding in the fourth innings had been 'beyond praise'.

Financially the festival was a huge success. The profit for the nine days of play exceeded £600 for only the third time in the event's history. This enabled the ground to completely discharge its outstanding war debt of £418 and contribute to a tidy bank balance of £350, bringing a glorious end to the first-class programme for the season.

The 1919 County Championship

The County Championship had now concluded. On the credit balance, a championship of sorts had been re-established. On the debit side it was a disjointed affair. Two-day matches led to a high number of draws. Players frequently did not leave the field of play until 7.30pm, with barely enough time to wash and eat before undertaking a journey to their next venue. Jack Hobbs recalled the season with dismay: 'It was hard work, and both cricketers and public soon got fed up with the new arrangement. After a 7.30 finish, by the time one had dressed and dined, it was too late to go anywhere.' The schedule particularly affected players whose fixture secretaries had managed a full programme. Wilfred Rhodes, whose Yorkshire side had arranged 26 matches, recalled, 'we had to dash away to catch the train and snatch what sleep we could'.

The two-day experiment, and the decision to decide the Championship positions based on the percentage of wins of matches played, 'robbed the Championship of much of its significance' according to *Wisden*. The result went to the wire, with Kent's inability to force a win at Lord's against Middlesex handing the title to Yorkshire; 'the actual result was all for the best' for *Wisden*, as the Tykes had played 28 matches to Kent's 14.

Nevertheless, spectators had rolled up to various matches in generally greater numbers than before the war. This provided a stepping stone for a more familiar county season for 1920 and beyond. The AIF matches were among the best-attended of the season, reigniting the interest of existing cricketing aficionados and introducing fans to the great game. All while providing a decent boost to depleted county coffers.

Had the AIF matches against the counties been included in a notional Championship, the Australians would have finished second in the table behind Yorkshire and just ahead of Kent. However, the number of three-day matches afforded to the tourists made a positive result more likely.

Wilfred Rhodes confirmed his transition from outstanding bowler, to all-rounder, to specialist opening batsman thence back to premier bowler by heading the national averages, his 164 wickets costing just 14.42 runs apiece. His pre-eminence was emblematic of the strong role the pre-war veterans had played in proceedings. George Gunn (63.08), Patsy Hendren (61.29) and Jack Hobbs (60.32) led the batting averages (more than 20 innings). Counties generally opted for the known qualities of their established players, rather than take risks with men who had experienced virtually no cricketing development over the past four summers. This hesitancy to take risks to discover new talent, along with resistance to playing 'England' matches on the AIF tour probably contributed to the first ever 5-0 whitewash in Test history in 1920/21, and the chaotic 1921 English Ashes side that experimented with 30 players to lose the five-Test series 3-0.

Chapter 22

Farewell

XVI of Mitcham

The Cricket Green, Mitcham on 13 September 1919
Result: Australian Imperial Forces won by six wickets

IT WAS fitting that the team tasked with rebuilding cricket should play their final match at the oldest continuously used ground in the world, the Cricket Green at Mitcham, where flannelled fools have plied their trade since 1685. The adjacent hotel The Cricketers was a base of operations for a number of 19th-century Australian tours, staying at the pub and practising on the Green. Hosting the AIF XI was former Mitcham captain and driving force of the tour Howard Lacy, captaining a XVI in a one-day benefit match for the Mitcham groundsman Harry Histed.

Surrey CCC assisted with the organisation of the match and four of their players were advertised as playing: JB Hobbs, A. Sandham, Dennis Sullivan and H. Strudwick. Hobbs and Strudwick did not take the field, however. Burnett Bullock would make his first-class county debut in 1921, and Albert Weyer would play for the second division Surrey side. Most of the rest of the Mitcham side are anonymous to history, with the notable exceptions of AIF XI member William Stirling, Lacy himself, and the man who had been Lacy's assistant and was to take over the management of the team from Lacy for the South African and Australian legs of the tour, Ernie Cameron.

Ernie Cameron

Ernie Cameron had been a star Australian Rules footballer before the war, winning a premiership with Essendon FC in 1911, and club best and fairest in 1911 and 1912. He broke his leg in the 1912 preliminary final, which Essendon won, but lost the following week's Grand Final in no small amount to being without their best player. The injury ended Cameron's playing career.

Cameron enlisted in the urgency of the middle of 1915, and was sent to Egypt, where he played in some cricket matches, including one with future AIF (and Lacy's XI) team member William Stirling. In 1917 he played for Lacy's XI in a charity match and for the AIF HQ in a match against Harrow. Cameron was mentioned in connection to the tour from the very start, even though his sporting fame was in the football arena, not cricket. This is likely because he had management experience as Essendon FC secretary for several years before his enlistment. Sam Michael, the journalist *Onlooker* who wrote so much in the lead-up to the tour and was a former team-mate in the Victorian colts football team, said of Cameron: 'He remains the same glad, open-hearted, unselfish sportsman, an ideal character for a manager of men … He has been a moving force behind the scenes, and it was due in a large measure to his resourcefulness and judgement that the team achieved such a measure of success and popularity.'

Although not with the AIF XI for the entire tour – for example, we know he was playing with Oldfield in the match against Trinity and New Colleges at Oxford in which Oldfield was discovered – Cameron was seconded to the team in July and was with them from that point onwards. He took over team management for the Scottish trips, when Lacy stayed in London. His statistics from the match – a duck with the bat and 0-49 with the ball – suggest management was the appropriate place for him in the side. Lacy, however, top-scored with 39 to help his side to a round 200 in their only innings in the one-day match. For the Australians Trenerry took five wickets and Gregory seven.

The AIF did not take long to get the required runs, thanks largely to 85 from Gregory and 61 from 'C. Smith' – whose precise identity is unknown, but it is likely the CR Smith who attends the farewell dinner two days later. Whoever he is, he has the privilege of being the last AIF wicket taken on English soil in 1919, drawing to a conclusion a popular and successful tour.

In 2019 the Cricket Green once again saw Mitcham CC take on an Australian XI in a match to mark the 100th anniversary of the AIF XI.

The final official function for the AIF XI came on Monday, 13 September with a dinner put on by *Wisden,* hosted by Lord Harris at the Café Monico. Many who had a hand in the tour were in attendance: joining Harris from the cricketing establishment were Plum Warner, Howard Lacy and Frank Jackson. There were multiple members of the top ranks of the AIF in attendance, including: Lt. Col. TS Woodburn CBE –

Chief Commissioner Australian Comforts Fund; Lt. Col. CV Watson DSO – Commanding Officer of 58th Battalion at Hamel and Amiens, for which he was awarded the DSO, newly appointed provost marshal AIF HQ at the time, and on the board for the Inter-Allied Games; Brigadier General C.H. Jess GMG DSO – the Commandant of AIF HQ in London who was just about to take over all of General Monash's roles, particularly Director General Repatriation, and would take over from Gen. Birdwood as General Commanding Officer AIF; Lt. Col. N. Marshall DSO, who fought in many important battles during the war, eventually getting two bars on his DSO. He was on the ASCB in 1919, where his main duty was coaching the championship-winning eight in the Henley Regatta. The Australian Minister of Defence, Senator George Pearce, had a seat of honour next to Lacy. Sir Marcus Samuel, the former Lord Mayor of London and the founder of what is now Shell Oil also sat at the head table. Gen. Birdwood was unable to attend due to other commitments.

In addition to the powerful were many of the best cricketers the team had met along the way, including: the Hon. Lionel Tennyson, the Reverend Frank Gillingham, George Griffiths, Jack Hearne, George Gunn, Patsy

Hendren, Jack Hobbs, Frank Woolley and Wally Hardinge.

The final group of attendees were from the media. At the head table with the guests of honour were Lord Burnham (Harry Levy-Lawson), MP and proprietor of the *Daily Telegraph*, and Maj. Philip Trevor, correspondent for the *Daily Telegraph* who travelled with MCC on the 1907/08 tour and published a diary of the tour. Representatives from several news outlets including the *Australian Press Association*, *Sporting Life*, and *The Times* were given seats on the outer.

The guests dined on oysters and turtle soup and enjoyed an accompaniment by the Imperial Orchestra who performed classics like *La Boheme*, war tunes like *Colonel Bogey March*, and contemporary hits from the West End like *Monsieur Beaucaire*. The after-dinner speeches and toasts fit the standard form for the time, starting with the king, before moving on to honour almost everyone in attendance: the AIF XI, *Wisden*, the press, MCC and Lord Harris amongst them. The toasts served to reinforce the purpose and values of the tour. Lord Harris praised Collins as captain, and expressed a debt of gratitude on behalf of the entire country towards the AIF for their 'invaluable services rendered', noting that the anxieties surrounding whether the public would return to cricket were 'happily unnecessary'. He concluded by noting the role cricket played in cementing the bonds of empire.

With all matches and official duties over, the historical record goes quiet on the lads' last week in London. It appears they guested with friends and acquaintances and prepared themselves for the still long journey back home to Australia. The guns had long been silent, but for the AIF XI service was not over.

Chapter 23

South Africa

WITH THE British leg of the tour over, cricket revived, fillips provided and finances secured, the AIF XI boarded the troopship HMT *Ascanius* – carrier of many an Australian soldier to and from the war – to at last follow their comrades home via the Cape of Good Hope. The departure time from London was at 'the witching hour', making the goodbye a rather subdued affair, with just a few friends and well-wishers and a solitary member of the press in attendance. Some of the players, making the most of their remaining hours in London, came to Paddington Station directly from the theatre. From there it was a train down to Devonport to board the *Ascanius* for their journey to Cape Town.

Before the AIF XI would dock in Cape Town, an MCC committee meeting at Lord's decided conclusively that while England would be unable to host an Australian side in 1920, they would be willing to tour Australia at the conclusion of next season's Championship for the Australian summer of 1920/21 and would welcome an Australian side in 1921.

For most returning soldiers, the stopover in South Africa was a brief shore leave in Cape Town. However, the AIF XI's shore leave was a further two months of cricket across South Africa; visiting Cape Town, Natal and Johannesburg, with the highlight of the tour two four-day games against a full-strength South African side. Minutes of South African Cricket Association (SACA) meetings show they had been trying to arrange a tour since December 1918 when such a prospect was still mostly whispers. However, given the AIF did not have the justification of providing a 'fillip' for South African cricket, funding would have to come from the local cricket community. As such, by August of 1919 when the details needed to be settled, SACA enthusiasm had waned – they were completely broke – but the Border and Western Province Cricket Unions were prepared to move forward without the national association. This brought the rest of the provinces on board and contact was made with the South African High Commissioner in London to speak with AIF authorities to organise a tour.

With just the two provincial cricket unions offering financial support, additional assistance was sought from mining magnate Sir Abe Bailey. Bailey had long been associated with Cecil Rhodes in both business and politics and had taken Rhodes' place in many facets of South African society, including the seat of Barkly West in the Cape Colony Legislative Assembly. This leg of the tour was much less about goodwill between nations and much more about Abe Bailey's prestige. Bailey was already a 'Randlord' – an unofficial title for one of the extremely rich mining bosses monopolising South African mineral wealth, named after the first great gold strike at the Witswatersrand, and known for their opulent houses in the Johannesburg suburb of Parktown.

Like most of the Randlords, Bailey was keen to legitimise his wealth with an actual title, and an Australian cricket tour was a perfect advertisement for his freshly awarded baronetcy. Bailey, along with Natal, Western Province and now Transvaal, provided a total guarantee for the tour: all travel, accommodation, tips, and other expenses would be covered, along with an allowance of £1 per day for 14 players and one manager, to be paid on top of the players' AIF wages. In the end, the tour profits and the guarantees provided by the provinces more than covered the tour and returned some profits to the provincial unions, with enough left over to award honorariums to the Australian players and manager. Bailey did not have to cough up a single pound, resulting in a very cheap goodwill campaign for the wily Randlord.

The state of South African cricket was not up to that of England or Australia before the war. Rapid improvement in the 20 years prior to the Triangular Tournament of 1912 led to high hopes that a third competitive side was entering the Test arena. However, the Triangular Tournament dashed those hopes, and the state of post-war South African cricket the AIF encountered on their tour somewhat confirmed it.

Cricket in South Africa had been disrupted even more than in England or Australia, and if the talent pool in 1913/14 had grown shallow, by 1919 it was nearly dry. Despite sending far fewer troops to the war – about 250,000 compared to more than 400,000 from Australia and around five million from Britain – seven South African Test players lost their lives in the war, while England lost four, and Australia only lost Tibby Cotter.

Of the South African Test casualties, Gordon White and Reggie Schwarz had been stalwarts in teams around the turn of the century and arguably would have been well past their best by the time the Australians toured. However, the loss of young up-and-coming fast bowlers Claude Newberry and Bill Lundie, both of whom had shown promise on England's tour of 1913/14, would be sorely felt in 1919. Also missing from the South African line-up was Herbie Taylor. Taylor was South Africa's second-highest run-getter in the Triangular Tournament of 1912, and the highest run-scorer of either side in England's tour of 1913/14, despite the South Africans losing the series 4-0.

He had also played in some of the charity matches during the war, including the England v Dominions game in 1918, and had also already played against the AIF XI in their first match against LG Robinson's side. Awarded the Military Cross for his services as a pilot in the war, he stayed on in England to play a season in the Air Force Rugby League with Blackheath. Taylor would go on to captain South Africa and be one of their greatest Test players. Even at the time he was recognised by Neville Cardus as 'one of the six greatest batsmen of the post-Grace period' and 'one of the finest batsmen living' by Jack Davis.

Things started hopefully for the locals. The first match against the strongest side in South Africa, Western Province, at Newlands in Cape Town finished in a nail-biting draw. Having slightly outscored the Australians in the first innings, Western Province set a fourth-innings target of 199. Five Australian batsmen failed to reach double figures, and the tourists scraped home with only two wickets to spare.

Next it was up to Johannesburg to meet Transvaal at the Wanderers ground. Here, consistency was key. Without any standout individual efforts, the Australians posted 392. In reply, Charles Frank and Billy Zulch put on a 99-run second-wicket stand in a total of 245 to leave them well behind, but in with a sniff of not embarrassing themselves. Not to be outdone, Gregory and Trenerry combined to make Australia's second-wicket partnership 138 runs, on the way to a total of 222. Unfortunately, the pair spent most of the final day's play doing this, leaving nowhere near enough time for Transvaal to score the 370 runs, or Australia to take the ten wickets, needed for victory.

The side then travelled to the Lord's ground in Durban. Natal, being the least developed of the three cricketing provinces, were no match, going down by 310 runs. The second match at Pietermaritzburg ended with an AIF victory by an innings and 42 runs, where a third day was not needed. It made sense then, that for the next match against Natal Colleges the home side were allowed to field a XV – this 'against the odds' match harking back to the days of the great touring professional sides of Clarke, Lillywhite and Wisden.[33] Being a one-day match in a time before playing one innings each had caught on, and the idea of limiting the overs had even been thought up, there was never going to be a result – although the Australians needed just 48 overs to despatch the students. One used to university matches played at that other Lord's may expect the side to be bristling with the next generation of talent. Indeed, in the side was future Test player Ivan Siedle. However, beyond that,

---

33 A relic from a time when cricket was much more orientated to the gambler, an 'against the odds' match pitches an XI against a larger side put together to balance the odds. Usually a XV, XVI, or a XXII, all members of the larger side would bat, and frequently all 15 or 16 would field, but a side of 22 would often put 11 to 16 on the field.

the most notable aspect of the team is how few players ever bothered the cricket records again. Victor Harrison would play 30 first-class matches for Natal, and Maurice Pennington 13, but for the other 13 players this would be their only taste of top-flight cricket.

It was then back aboard the train for the long journey to Johannesburg. Those days of the tight schedules but short journeys back in England must have been a sweet memory. The warm-up game against Transvaal again ended with a dominant Australian victory by an innings. Then it was time for the main event – the first four-day match against a full-strength South Africa.

Although never even considered as Test status, you could not have convinced a South African cricket fan of this in 1919. As far as they were concerned the AIF XI was the best Australia had to offer. South Africa would provide likewise. If two Test-playing nations met each other on the field with full-strength sides in a four-day match, then surely this was a Test.

It had been a long drought for the South Africans. The glory days of Schwarz, Faulkner, and Vogler ripping googlies on the matting wickets of 1905/06 and 1909/10 that saw the South Africans defeat the English for their first series victories were long behind them. Their solitary win on the 1910/11 tour of Australia had been their last, the only rained-out draw of the tri-tournament being compounded by a 4-0 loss in the five-Test series against a visiting England in 1913/14. But back at home, on the matting wickets, perhaps?

The Australian side looked the favourites, yet the resistance shown in the first game by Western Province had to hold out some hope that with a full-strength side Capetonians were at least in with a chance. And full strength it was. Only two of the XI never played a Test match, although Alfred Cooper, Doug Meintjes and Cec Dixon would play just a single series, and George Hearne (no, not that one, or that one, but yes, nephew and grandson of the English Test greats) only represented South Africa three times. However, the remaining five were all members of at least the 1913/14 side.

Afrikaner Jimmy Blanckenberg played in 18 Tests for South Africa before heading to England in 1925, where he would play in various professional leagues, before migrating to Germany sometime after the rise of Hitler. He officially died in Berlin in 1955, but rumours have him as fleeing for South America after the war. Philip Hands was more representative of the other white group in South Africa; the English. Son of the Mayor of Cape

Town Sir Harry Hands KBE, he was a Rhodes Scholar and served with distinction in the war, being awarded the Distinguished Service Order and the Military Cross. His brother, Reginald, was also a Test player, but had been killed in the war. Sir Harry's act of remembering his son's death on Armistice Day with two minutes of silence is credited as founding that solemn practice.

Billy Zulch had been a promising up and comer when the war broke out, his most notable performances coming on the 1910/11 tour of Australia where he was the second-highest scorer for the South Africans in the five-Test series. However, by 1919, he was reaching the end of his career and he had just a few more seasons in him. Wicketkeeper Tommy Ward had a credible 23-Test career, although his most notorious statistic comes from his debut Test against Australia in 1912. Twice in the match he walked on to the field to face up to a hat-trick ball, both times falling for a golden duck, giving him the ignominious achievements of having scored a king pair on debut and being involved in both hat-tricks that make up the only time two hat-tricks have been taken in a Test match.

This leaves Dave Nourse, the backbone of the South African team for nearly 20 years at this point. Born in

England, he travelled on military service to South Africa in 1895, and never left – cricket tours aside. He played in every South African Test match between 1902 and 1923, when, aged 45, he retired from Test cricket. Along the way he picked up his maiden Test ton with his 111 against Australia in 1921, still the oldest player to do so. Nourse played the majority of his prime career up until 1925 with Natal, but even after his Test retirement, and departure from Natal, he would play first-class cricket – mostly with Western Province – until 1936, when he retired from first-class cricket at 58, capping off a great career with a solid 55 against the Australians.

South Africa
First 'Test'

Old Wanderers, Johannesburg on 21–22 and 24–25 November 1919
Result: Australian Imperial Forces won by eight wickets

It rained heavily the night before the first 'Test' at the Wanderers. Although these were still the days before covered wickets, they were also before the days of turf pitches in South Africa, with matting wickets still the standard. Although some dampness would improve a matting wicket, unlike the proverbial 'sticky wicket' of damp turf, it still provided for a dead outfield. On winning the toss Billy Zulch decided to bat, taking advantage of the damp matting, and perhaps deciding that making all 11 Australians spend the first day slopping around in the mud would give the locals the edge.

It was the wrong choice. Zulch and opening partner Hearne faced an opening spell from Gregory and Collins bowling to four slips. A dead outfield made scoring on the ground difficult, although Hearne could find the boundary with a drive or cut, and Zulch found the fence 'around the corner' with some leg glances. With the total on 36 – and the morning's showers turning to rain – Hearne edged one through to Oldfield off Collins, and the stout resistance provided thus far collapsed, a rain delay only yielding a short respite. All ten South African wickets fell for just 91 runs – Gregory and Collins bowling every over and equally sharing the wickets – the home side setting a first-innings total of 127.

The Australians quickly cleaned up the last two South African wickets before coming in to bat in glorious weather on day two that would continue for the rest of the match. The Wanderers outfield returned to its regular 'brick' status, and scoring was considerably easier – at least for Herbie Collins. The opener batted all day, and on into day three, posting a massive double ton, the only notable score in the Australian innings of 441. Collins spent every second over on day one running in to bowl on a sodden field, taking 5-52, and then six hours batting on day two, most of the Australian innings on day three, and still bowled another 20 overs, taking 2-35.

A 324-run first-innings deficit seemed to have put the match out of reach for the South Africans, but Billy Zulch had other ideas, scoring a valiant 135. However, with the exception of Ward – who scored 62 in an exemplary keeper's middle-order knock – the locals were overwhelmed, with no one else able to get out of the 20s. This was still enough to force the Australians in to bat a second time. They chased down the 47 runs required in the tenth over, losing two wickets along the way, but fortunately for Collins he was not required to step out of the dressing room again.

Second 'Test'

Old Wanderers, Johannesburg on 29–30 November, 1–2 December 1919
Result: Australian Imperial Forces won by eight wickets

It would have made sense for the second 'Test' to be played at Newlands in Cape Town. Western Province and Transvaal were the two cricketing powerhouses in the nation, akin to the domination New South Wales and Victoria enjoyed in Australia, with hints of the North/South rivalry in England. However, it seems this rivalry soured during the organisation of the tour. In the lead-up to the Australians' visit it was Transvaal who were hesitant, and Western Province who were the keener. However, by the time the second four-day fixture had to be set, Western Province were complaining about the exorbitant guarantee SACA were demanding and refused to pay it.

They already had a few matches against the AIF XI set for the Western Province XI, at a lower guarantee. The administrators in Cape Town saw no advantage hosting what was now spoken of in the local papers as 'fake' Tests – which they were – but the shift is worth noting. Exactly why the mood changed would be a question for the long dead journalists writing the articles in the *Cape Times*, but it should be noted this was a period of growing antipathy between the Western Province Cricket Union and Transvaal Cricket Union as power over cricket was shifting to the booming mining province, with its newly minted Randlord patrons, none more than Abe Bailey.

There was some attempt by local boards to get the second four-day match played in Griqualand or Natal, but in the end no one could match the financial power of Transvaal. So again the crowds streamed into the Wanderers. Although the defeat had been heavy in the first match, the South African first innings – and Collins' batting exploits – aside, there was much to be hopeful for. If the home side could bat like they did in the second innings, and bowl like they did for much of the match, it was game on.

Zulch once again won the toss and decided to go in on a damp mat, this time with Ward as his partner as Hearne was out with an injury. Collins and Docker opened the bowling for the Australians. Things started slowly: two runs off eight overs. Collins and Docker were bowling tight, but not getting chances. Collins brought on Gregory and 'The Streak' started a barrage of bouncers and the 'leg theory' which was becoming popular at the time and which would culminate in the infamous 'Bodyline' series. A hit to the thigh had Ward down for five minutes, but he was able to resume, albeit somewhat cautious of the bowling now.[34] Not long after,

34 That Ward was hit on the 'thigh' is a direct quote from a match report. For this to result in being laid out for five minutes – around a team just returned from a war – either speaks to the meteoric pace of Gregory, or the decorum of the journalist.

Zulch was put down in the slips. The fragile pair were saved by the lunch bell, and South Africa walked into the rooms at the first break on a hopeful 68/0.

The news was out and by the end of the lunch break the ground was packed to the rafters – and beyond. After a few sighters, Zulch drove well beyond mid-on and sauntered through for a single, leaving Ward to face Gregory. Ward skied the first delivery and was easily taken by Collins. 76/1. Frank came to the wicket, and immediately turned back around, stumps akimbo. 76/2. Zulch was joined by Nourse; if any pair could save the innings it was this combination. After a few maidens to steady themselves, Zulch was back in the pavilion, having also been pouched by Collins. 76/3. Enter Hands. Almost immediately he was in trouble, dropped in the slips by Collins off Gregory. The captain was able to quickly redeem himself, trapping Nourse lbw. 83/4. The South Africans must have breathed a sigh of relief when the heavens opened around 2:30, forcing a suspension in the play, and giving the mat a nice soak to make it behave a little bit better.

Tancred joined Hands out in the middle and saw off the interrupted Collins over. Two balls later Tancred was joined by Meintjes. 87/5. The next ball it was Davies' turn to join Tancred. 87/6. Tancred managed to bat out the innings to finish on 16 not out, but the closest he came to having a partner was Cox batting at No.11. The two managed to raise the score from 99/9 to 117, the Australians taking all ten South African wickets between lunch and tea. From excited exuberance to desperate despair in the space of a session. But as any good cricket lover knows, you can't judge a wicket until both teams have batted. Fortunately, those in attendance on the first day were able to go home with this knowledge, the Australians ending the day just three runs behind, with eight wickets in hand.

If the Australians' big first innings in the first match was a solo performance, this time they brought the full symphony. Not a single centurion, but contributions all the way down the line on the way to 456 left Australia in a dominant position heading into the second half of the match. Not helping matters was Ward being unable to keep, although he was in the field, seemingly still hurting from Gregory's attentions the day before. Even worse, Zulch was not even on the ground, having been involved in a car accident during the lunch break.

In the South African reply, Tancred, Nourse and Blanckenberg all scored notable half-centuries, but along with Zulch, Hands was also out due to a leg injury he sustained earlier in the match. As such, the South Africans at 210/8 had to declare their innings, still over 100 runs from forcing the Australians to bat a second time.

All that remained for the Australians were two matches in Cape Town, one against Western Province, and one against a XV from the Western Province Colleges. The first match had to compete against a variety of other sports for the interest of the Cape Town crowd with racing, athletics, bowls and golf tournaments occurring on the same day. In light of this, the crowds were still thought of as decent, but they were down significantly on previous contests of similar stature. That the other sports drew people away is undeniable, but it does prompt one to think whether the talking down of the quality of the Australian side to take away from the Johannesburg matches as 'Tests' may have had something to do with it. Even so, the first match against Western Province on arrival had been the closest the Australians had come to losing, something those in Cape Town mentioned with pride in light of the disastrous results in Johannesburg.

The first day's play saw an exhilarating struggle between bat and ball, the Australians posting 269 while the home side acquitted themselves admirably in the field. However, any hope of this spurring the crowds to attend on day two were dashed by the weather. The innovative decision of the Newlands groundstaff to cover the wicket during the downpours also took away the benefit Western Province would gain from batting on a damp mat. This was not a perfect art yet, and although they kept the wicket dry, the water pooling off the tarpaulin created mud holes in the field. This all had the effect of delaying play until 2pm when the Western Province opening pair went out to the field to resume the overnight score of 30/0. The next hour was a disaster as they lost six wickets for just 38 runs. GP Taylor and Blanckenberg were able to steady the ship somewhat, but they were still unable to see out the shortened day, falling for 153 before sending the Australians back in.

Collins opened with determination, losing Trenerry along the way for 1, to leave Australia at 29/1 at stumps, 145 runs in the lead. The following day they raced to 164/6 before declaring and setting Western Province 281 for victory. But the declaration came too late. Despite an admirable attempt to chase down the Australian score, time won the day, leaving Western Province 140 runs adrift with three wickets to spare. Although outmatched,

Western Province at least now had the bragging rights of being the only side to push the Australians on the tour, even if the home crowds were not able to see a full-strength South African side make the attempt.

The final match against the Western Province Colleges was much like that against Natal. The two innings one-day match was naturally drawn, the Australians winning on first innings 115 to 344, with no future talent presenting themselves on the field that day. It was followed by a smoking concert to bid farewell to the players, with the usual round of mutual congratulations. In particular, Collins assured South Africans their cricket was in a good state, with good organisation and promising youngsters coming through. All they lacked was a spin bowler who could really turn one, which had been the South African speciality to this point. They would also need a quick with a bit of extra pace if they were to have any hope on Australian wickets.

The next day it was all aboard the HMT *Aeneas* for the trip – finally – home to Australia. At this stage, the players did not know if they had played their last game together, and whether the return home was really returning home, or just the beginning of another tour.

Although not intended as a 'fillip' for South African cricket, in time the AIF tour, along with the Test tour of 1921, were recognised by Herbie Collins as 'sav[ing] South African cricket when it was dying'.

Chapter 24

Australia

THE PLAYERS embarked the HMT *Aeneas* at Cape Town on the evening of 18 December to begin the steam home. Joining them on board were about 1,200 other repatriating Diggers, and Sister Hilda Hope McMaugh. Sister McMaugh served with the Australian Army Nursing Service during the war and, while awaiting repatriation in England, became the first Australian woman to get a pilot's licence (although the licence was not recognised in Australia). Incredibly, her qualification flight was captured on film and is available to watch on British Pathé.

As far as the AIF XI were concerned the tour was over – the war was over – and they must have been looking forward to returning to their families. However, behind the scenes, after seeing both the playing and propaganda successes of the team in England and South Africa, the decision was taken to organise a home series as well, with matches against Victoria, New South Wales and Queensland as definite. The players were informed via a ship-to-shore radio message as they made their way across the Indian Ocean.

There was a plan in motion to get the team to stop in Western Australia for a few matches. Jas Farley, the secretary of the Western Australian Cricket Association International and Interstate Committee, initially sent the request for games to the Australian Board of Control. This is symbolic of the confusion surrounding the organisation of the tour, especially given the request was made in November 1919. The ABC reminded Farley it was the Defence Department who were organising the tour and so a request was sent to Senator Pearce, who advised there would be 'no objection provided the transport *Aeneas* calls at Western Australia'. Although they did indeed stop in Fremantle, no matches were organised.

Here the players had another Spanish flu scare. On board was a 'cot case'; a soldier incapacitated with the disease. Before the ship could dock, a tender went to collect the man. However, 'owing to the heavy swell the patient was kept on the gangway some considerable time, causing him much bumping and pain'. Eventually, the *Aeneas* pulled up beside the wharf, allowing the 40 or so Western Australian troops back into the arms of loved ones not seen in years, while the rest of the troops were allowed down to the YMCA for some shore leave. The cricketers themselves had many media outlets and well-wishers waiting for them.

However, for Collins, the first concern on arrival in Fremantle was the cricket scores.

> 'Have you any scores of the Sheffield Shield games?'
>
> The speaker was a sturdy looking Digger, but with that look of alertness and keenness which suggested a cricketing instinct. On being informed that New South had beaten South Australia, and in turn had been beaten by Victoria, he heaved a sigh of relief.
>
> 'As long as Victoria beats New South,' he concluded, 'the other matches don't matter'.
>
> It was mentioned afterwards that the speaker was AW Lampard, of Victoria.

> Herbie Collins summed up the tour:
>
> 'Do you know,' remarked Collins, 'this trip has been a record as far as the social side is concerned. Everywhere we have gone the team has been feted and made much of, that we do not know where we are half the time. I, for one, will be glad to see the finish of it.'

At which stage the interview was interrupted as Collins had to reply to a telegram from Melbourne from Ernie Bean, secretary of the Victorian Cricket Association, about the match to be played in Melbourne.

The *Aeneas*' next stop was Adelaide. The South Australian Cricket Association had sent a delegate to Melbourne to organise a match with the AIF XI. Unfortunately, however, their date of arrival in Adelaide clashed with South Australia's away Sheffield Shield games for the season and the team was off being thoroughly trounced by the eastern states. Some felt it was 'an admission of weakness' that a second XI could not be organised to meet the AIF XI, but on paper it seems likely such a match would have been one-sided in the extreme; the South Australians lost every Sheffield Shield match between the 1919/20 and 1923/24 seasons.

The team eventually left the *Aeneas* for good when they arrived in Melbourne on Saturday, 10 January 1920. A welcome ceremony was held at Scott's hotel where they were greeted by politicians, cricketers and the general public. But the tour was not over; the eastern states all awaited a visit from the soldier-cricketers.

Victoria

Melbourne Cricket Ground, Melbourne on 16–17 and 19 January 1920
Result: Australian Imperial Forces won by six wickets

Their first match was against Victoria. The Victorian team had several players who probably would not have had a first-class career were it not for the disruption of the war. However, they also had some of their Test players who did not fight in the war. Edgar Mayne had a long first-class career with first South Australia and then Victoria, and also played a part in the Triangular Tour and the 1921/22 tour of South Africa. Ted McDonald had played for Victoria since 1911 after transferring from Tasmania. After the war he played in the first two post-war Ashes series and the 1921/22 tour of South Africa. His performances in the 1921 Ashes earnt him *Wisden* Cricketer of the Year in 1922. He returned to

England that year and played for Lancashire County Cricket Club in the Championship and Nelson in the Lancashire League until the early 1930s.

Jack Ryder was yet to play Test cricket, but had already had several impressive seasons for Victoria, although 1919/20 was the worst Shield season of his career. His early performances the following season were enough to earn him a call-up to the Test squad for the home Ashes series, becoming a regular for the next five Test series, eventually playing in 20 Test matches. Finally, the Victorian captain was the 'Governor General' himself, Warwick Armstrong, who would be Australia's Test captain for the next two series, despite already being 41 with over 20 seasons of first-class cricket behind him.

Armstrong and Mayne got off to good starts to have the Vics 49/0 before both fell in quick succession. From then on the home side were barely able to get a ten-run partnership together, Gregory's deadly bowling capturing seven wickets for a meagre 22 runs. To see such a bowler – who could also bat, let us not forget – dismantle the side which just the week before had beaten the strong New South Welshmen must have whetted the cricketing appetites of the MCG crowd, even as their side fell apart.

At 40/3 in response, it seemed like there was a match afoot. However, Willis and Pellew combined for a 100-run partnership to move the first-innings score past that of the Victorians, the former on the way to 111. Lampard and Gregory, batting seven and eight, both put in cameos to guide the tail to 311, nearly 200 runs to the good. In the second Victorian innings the opener Mayne managed a half-century as the top order collapsed around him. With the score 97/6, forcing a second AIF innings looked a long way off. The tail wagged, however, and dragged the Vics close to the total. The ninth wicket fell with 13 runs still needed and the match looked over, but Ellis and Carlton stubbornly stayed at the crease, their tenth-wicket partnership yielding 88 runs to at least give the bowlers a target to aim at. However, it was nowhere near enough as the AIF gathered the required runs needed to seal the match in under an hour.

Queensland

Brisbane Cricket Ground, Woolloongabba, Brisbane on 24 and 26–27 January 1920
Result: Match drawn

The side then had four days to travel the 2,000km to Brisbane to meet Queensland. They arrived at Brisbane

Central Station the night before the match, and were met by a large and enthusiastic crowd, supported by the 'Diggers' Band and a military guard of honour. They were then the guests of honour at a dinner hosted by the mayor of Brisbane, and the secretary of the Queensland Cricket Association.

Most of the AIF XI had likely already met the Queensland skipper for the match, Warrant Officer James Sheppard. Sheppard had been one of the names mentioned during the early talk surrounding the tour and had indeed gone along to the selection trials. Although he did not make the team, he remained attached to the Sports Control Board until he left England in August of 1919. He was probably unlucky to have been left out; if the ABC had been in control of selection it is likely he would have been picked on the basis of interstate parochialism alone.

The AIF won the toss and went into bat. Although Collins and Gregory put up some opposition, Queensland required just a touch over 40 overs to have them all out for 215. The Queensland batsmen were able to stay in the match on the first day, finishing at stumps on 96/3. The bowling attack found their form on day two, as the AIF quickly took the rest of the wickets to have the home side out for 146. Collins' opening score of 135 showed the Queenslanders it was not all the pitch's doing, and able support from Taylor (67) helped the AIF along to 319/5 when they declared, nearly 390 runs ahead, and sent the opposition in to see out the day. The locals were looking shaky at 144/6 when a typical Brisbane thunderstorm rolled in during the afternoon and ended the match in a draw. During the match, at 4:05 on days one and three, all the players on the ground formed a square and a bugler played 'The Last Post' as a memorial to those who had fallen. The large crowd that had shown up to see the AIF XI play joined them in standing in silence.

New South Wales

Sydney Cricket Ground, Sydney on 31 January, 2–3 February 1920
Result: Australian Imperial Forces won by 203 runs

The final match of the tour was one of the biggest. The recent Victorian Sheffield Shield victory over the New South Welshmen had come as somewhat of a surprise, as New South Wales had been the pre-war cricketing powerhouse. This New South Wales team were no bunch of mugs either. Past or future Test cricketers Warren Bardsley, Sammy Carter, Stork Hendry, Tommy

Andrews, Alan Kippax and Arthur Mailey gave the feel of a 'those that did not serve' side to meet the 'those who served' AIF XI. Also in the New South Wales side were Ted Trenerry and Keith Docker, making two pairs of brothers reunited as adversaries on the Sydney Cricket Ground that day. And no doubt there were a flock of Gregorys in the stands to see the 'black sheep' of the family finally making good on his name in his home country, scoring a brilliant century to lead the AIF XI to 265 runs in their first knock.

In response, Bardsley and Hendry both passed 50 as New South Wales went into a slight first-innings lead of 14 runs, while Gregory underlined his all-round status with a five-fer, leaving the contest tightly balanced in the middle of the second day. Collins was having none of it and led from the front. After losing the first two wickets relatively cheaply he was joined at the crease by Gregory. The pair moved the score from 101/2 to 289/3 when Collins fell on 129, Gregory following him seven runs later when he was stumped by Carter on 102. A few other starts from several players were all the AIF XI needed to reach 395 and set New South Wales 382 for the victory with most of day three to get it. In the end the star-studded NSW line-up was not up to the task and only Tommy Andrews managed to reach a half-century, falling over 100 runs short of the target.

The Final Legacy

And so finally the Australian Imperial Forces XI were disbanded and allowed to return to civilian life, although the team was not officially demobilised until the end of March. On the impact of the tour the *Maitland Daily Mercury* put it thus:

> It was inevitable that when various sports were organised for the physical and moral benefit of the AIF men, pending the completion of their repatriation, that a cricket team would be formed, but it was never expected that the resultant organisation, without a single man of Test match calibre and experience, would have such a highly successful career as that which has just been terminated. Socially, as well as for its cricket, the AIF combination has worthily upheld the reputation of Anglo-British sportsmen.
>
> The camaraderie of cricket and the absence of snobbery in Australian sport was

> well illustrated by the loyalty of their chosen leader, despite the fact of his lower military rank. We are not much concerned about the popularity of cricket from a spectacular point of view, because we would much rather see a large number of players, and a small total of spectators than vice versa; but it would be well for our cricketers to note how popular AIF cricket was, because of the sparkling aggressive tactics of the batsmen, the splendid fielding, and especially the alertness of batsmen between the wickets. Lethargie and slovenly running between the wickets spoils many a match for the on-looker, and robs the teams concerned of many a run. We are glad to note what has been done by the AIF men to popularise the good old game, and hope that their example of cricket as it should be played will be an inspiration to our young cricketers, that will give post-war cricket the fillip it needs.

Australian cricket had recovered even before the AIF XI had returned. The Shield season of 1918/19 was a success, and now with the benefit of a successful English county season, particularly the performances of the AIF XI, there were none of the earlier anxieties around whether cricket would be back to its old place now the war was over. Large crowds reminiscent of pre-war numbers had attended the Victoria v NSW fixture in the weeks before the players' arrival home. That the select band of soldier-cricketers had held their own against England's best had Australian fans confident that once a full team of Australians were assembled, they would have no problems matching a full-strength England side, a fact well borne out by the results over the next few years.

For Australia, the true legacy of the AIF XI was held within the Australian cricket team itself. The core of the Australian side of the 1920s came from the AIF XI in the names of Collins, Taylor, Pellew, Oldfield and Gregory. The cost estimate of £2,000, made during the opening of the tour, was easily covered by gate receipts, to the point where the AIF XI were able to pay money back to the ASCB to fund other sports. The intensity in the field, so much a highlight of many of the games played on the tour, became a feature of the Australian sides to follow. Although the debate over player control was now well and truly lost to the board, the tensions surrounding rank and class during the tour – already anathema to Australian cricket – meant the idea of a hierarchy within the side itself was rejected for good.

The benefits for English cricket are clearer. Although it is likely cricket would have returned to its place as the grand old game, the crowds would have returned and English cricket would have rebuilt, the confusion surrounding selections for the 1921 Ashes series would have likely been deeper and lasted longer. What is not in dispute is the AIF XI drew a crowd wherever they went. As mentioned in the introduction, by the time of the armistice most county clubs in England were in serious financial trouble, especially those still operating largely on the 19th-century economic model of large support from a small number of wealthy patrons.

However, many of those clubs were in trouble *before* the war. When the larger organisations of MCC, Surrey, Yorkshire and Lancashire are removed, the entire county system was in trouble in 1914, with clubs on average around £800 in debt. Although many were able to rely on their wealthy supporters to pay down debt during the war, leaving an average balance of £0 in 1918, by the end of the 1919 season the average balance for these clubs was over £1,000 – all of it drawn from the 1919 season. For MCC it was almost *exactly* a return to normal. Gate receipts in 1919 were £5,003, compared to £5,005 in 1914, despite the dreaded 'entertainment tax' many were convinced was driving down crowds.

The true 'fillip' provided by the AIF XI was to these clubs. Not only did the large crowds fill empty coffers, but they provided the model for how a cricket club was to survive in the 20th century – by providing attractive and exciting cricket to entice ticket-paying spectators through the turnstiles.

Averages

The AIF XI played 28 first-class matches in England, with 12 wins, 12 defeats and four draws.

Batting

Name	*I*	*R*	*High Score*	*N.O.*	*Average*
CB Willis	44	1,652	156*	4	41.30
HL Collins	44	1,615	127	2	38.45
CE Pellew	40	1,260	195*	7	38.18
WA Oldfield	19	382	80*	7	31.83
JM Taylor	39	1,187	146	1	31.23
JM Gregory	36	942	115	4	29.43
WL Trennery	37	961	82	3	28.26
AW Lampard	35	821	112	3	25.65
JT Murray	34	793	133	1	24.03
CT Docker	17	214	52*	7	21.40
EA Bull	23	395	42	2	18.80
WS Stirling	35	538	62	3	16.81
EJ Long	19	110	14*	9	11.00
H. Love	2	2	2	0	1.00

Bowling

Name	*O*	*M*	*R*	*W*	*Average*
HL Collins	728.5	164	1,755	106	16.55
JM Gregory	830	124	2,383	131	18.16
CT Docker	200.2	35	576	27	21.33
WS Stirling	378.5	83	964	44	21.90
CW Winning	472.4	106	1,164	52	22.38
AW Lampard	519.2	72	1,627	69	23.57
WL Trennery	57.4	4	221	7	31.57
JT Murray	15	2	61	1	61.00

Bibliography

Altham, H.S., *A History of Cricket: From the Beginnings to the First World War* (London: George Allen & Unwin, 1962)

Astill, Edwin, *The Great War Diaries of Brigadier Alexander Johnston, 1914–1917* (Barnsley: Pen and Sword, 2007)

Allen, Dean, *Empire, War & Cricket in South Africa: Logan of Matjiesfontein* (South Africa: Penguin Random House South Africa, 2015)

Beardsall, Brian, *From the Stretford End: Official History of the Lancashire County Cricket Club* (London: Partridge Press, 1990)

Birley, Derek, *A Social History of English Cricket* (London: Aurum Press, 1999)

Bonnell, Max & Sprout, Andrew, *Tibby Cotter: Fast Bowler, Larrikin, ANZAC* (Walla Walla Press, 2017)

Bowen, Roland, *Cricket: A History of its Growth and Development throughout the World* (London: Eyre & Spottiswoode, 1970)

Bradbury, Anthony, *Frank Gillingham: Clerical Cricketer or Cricketing Clergyman?* (Bedford: Association of Cricket Statisticians and Historians, 2021)

Broadribb, Gerald, *The Croucher: A Biography of Gilbert Jessop* (London: Constable, 1974)

Burns, Michael, *A Flick of the Fingers: The Chequered Life and Career of Jack Crawford* (Worthing: Pitch Publishing Ltd, 2015)

Cardwell, Ronald L., *The A.I.F. Cricket Team* (NSW: R.L. Cardwell, 1980)

Chester, Frank, *How's that!* (London: Hutchinson, 1956)

Coldham, James P., *Lord Hawke: A Cricketing Legend* (London: I.B. Tauris, 2003)

Cross Standing, Percy, *Anglo-Australian Cricket 1862–1926* (London: Faber and Gwyer, 1926)

Croudy, Brian, *Herbert Wilfred Taylor* (Nottingham: Association of Cricket Statisticians and Historians, 2005)

Down, Michael, *Archie: A Biography of A.C. MacLaren* (London: George Allen & Unwin, 1981)

Edworthy, Niall, *Lord's: The Home of Cricket* (London: Virgin Books, 1999)

Evans, A.J, *The Escaping Club* (Harmondsworth.Penguin, 1943)

Frith, David, *Pageant of Cricket* (London: MacMillan, 1987)

Frith, David, *The Golden Age of Cricket, 1890–1914* (Guildford: Lutterworth Press, 1978)

Growden, Greg, *Cricketers at War: Cricket Heroes Who Fought for Australia in Battle* (Sydney: HarperCollins, 2019)

Hart, Peter, *1918: A Very British Victory* (London: Weidenfield and Nicholson, 2008)

Harte, Chris, *A History of Australian Cricket* (London: Deutsch, 1993)

Hignell, Andrew, *The History of Glamorgan County Cricket Club* (London: The History Press, 1988)

Hignell, Andrew, *Front Foot to Front Line: Welsh Cricket and the Great War* (Cardiff: Welsh Academic Press, 2017)

Hill, Alan, *Herbert Sutcliffe: Cricket Maestro* (London: Simon & Schuster, 1991)

Hobbs, Jack, *My Life Story* (London: The Star, 1935)

Howat, Gerald, *Plum Warner* (London: Unwin Hyman, 1983)

Jenkinson, Neil, *C.B. Llewellyn: A Study in Equivocation* (Cardiff: Association of Cricket Statisticians and Historians, 2012)

Lemmon, David, *Johnny Won't Hit Today: A Cricketing Biography of J.W.H.T. Douglas* (London: George Allen & Unwin, 1983)

Lemmon, David & Marshall, Mike, *Essex County Cricket Club: The Official History* (London: Heinemann, 1987)

Leveson Gower, Henry, *Off and On the Field* (London: Stanley Paul, 1953)

Lonsdale, Jeremy, *A Game Sustained: The Impact of the First World War on Cricket in Yorkshire, 1914–1920* (Bedford: Association of Cricket Statisticians and Historians, 2019)

Low, Robert, *WG Grace: An Intimate Biography* (London: Metro Publishing, 2004)

Macdonald, Lyn, *1915: The Death of Innocence* (London: Penguin, 1997)

McCrery, Nigel, *Final Wicket: Test and First Class Cricketers Killed in the Great War* (Barnsley, Pen & Sword, 2015)

McKinstry, Leo, *Jack Hobbs: England's Greatest Cricketer* (London: Yellow Jersey Press, 2011)

Murphy, Patrick, *'Tiger' Smith of Warwickshire and England* (Guildford: Lutterworth Press, 1981)

Musk, Stephen, *Lionel Robinson: Cricket at Old Buckenham* (Cardiff: Association of Cricket Statisticians and Historians, 2014)

Odendaal, André, *Cricket and Conquest: The History of South African Cricket Retold. Volume I, 1795–1914* (Cape Town: BestRed, 2016)

Oldfield, W.A, *Behind the Wicket* (London: Hutchinson & Co., 1938)

Oldfield, W.A., *The Rattle of the Stumps* (London: George Newnes Limited, 1954)

Paine, Philip & Norcross, Daniel, *The 48: A Tribute to the Men of Surrey CCC in the First World War* (Surrey CCC, 2018)

Parkinson, Justin, *Then Came Massacre: The Story of Maurice Tate, Cricket's Smiling Destroyer* (Durrington: Pitch Publishing, 2013)

Pardon, Sydney (ed.), *Wisden Cricketers' Almanack* (John Wisden & Company)

Pollard, Jack, *The Turbulent Years of Australian Cricket, 1893–1917* (NSW: Angus & Robertson, 1987)

Pollard, Jack, *The Complete Illustrated History of Australian Cricket*, Rev. ed (Ringwood, Vic.; New York, NY: Viking, 1995)

Pope, Mick, *Tragic White Roses: The Sad Story of Yorkshire Cricketers Alonzo Drake and Major Booth* (Privately Published, 1995)

Renshaw, Andrew (ed.), *Wisden on the Great War: The Lives of Cricket's Fallen, 1914–1918* (John Wisden & Co., 2014)

Robinson, Ray & Haigh, Gideon, *On top down under: Australia's cricket captains* (Adelaide: Wakefield, 1996)

Sandford, Christopher, *The Final Over: The Cricketers of 1914* (London: The History Press, 2015)

Scoble, Christopher, *Colin Blythe: Lament for a Legend* (Cheltenham: SportsBooks Limited, 2005)

Sissons, Ric, *The Players: A Social History of the Professional Cricketer* (London: Kingswood Press, 1988)

Stoddart, Brian, and Sandiford, Keith, eds., *The Imperial Game: Cricket, Culture, and Society, Studies in Imperialism* (Manchester: Manchester University Press, 1998)

Streeton, Richard, *P.G.H.Fender: A Biography* (London: Faber & Faber, 1981)

Swanton, E.W., *A History of Cricket: From the First World War to the Present Day* (London: George Allen & Unwin, 1962)

Tate, Maurice, *My Cricketing Reminiscences* (London: Stanley Paul, 1934)

Tennyson, Lionel, *Sticky Wickets* (London: Christopher Johnson, 1950)

Thomas, Andrew, *Pears 150: The Life and Times of Worcestershire County Cricket Club 1865–2014* (Worcestershire CCC, 2015)

Vamplew, Wray, *Pay Up and Play the Game: Professional Sport in Britain, 1875–1914* (Cambridge: Cambridge University Press, 1988)

Van Duinen, Jared, *The British World and an Australian National Identity: Anglo-Australian Cricket, 1860–1901* (London: Palgrave Macmillan Limited, 2017)

Whitington, R.S., *An Illustrated History of Australian Cricket* (Melbourne: Lansdowne, 1972)

Wilde, Simon, *England: The Biography* (London: Simon & Schuster, 2018)

Williams, Jack, *Cricket and England: A Cultural and Social History of the Inter-war Years* (London: Frank Cass, 1999)

Wynne-Thomas, Peter, *Arthur Carr: The Rise and Fall of Nottinghamshire's Bodyline Captain* (Chequered Flag Publishing, 2017)

Newspapers and Periodicals

The British Newspaper Archive and Trove Australia were the primary archives for this work, with additional assistance coming from University of Witwatersrand, Johannesburg. Please visit AnthonyCondon.com for a 'historically factional' tour diary, where you will find many of the articles used in the research for this book presented in the voice of a fictional journalist travelling with the team.

Index